THEY KNEW ME WHEN

An Improbable Memoir of a Poet

S.R. Lavin

Foreword by Rosa Sophia Godshall

Published by Lady June Press.
Printed in the United States of America.
Library of Congress Control Number:
ISBN-13: 979-8-218-64343-0
First Paperback Edition

"If you would like to be a citizen of the world
someone will remind you who you are.
You will be fortunate if it's in a nice way.
I always saw boxing as a sport.
I made a study of it."

— *Fred Lavin*

Roses are red, violets are blue,
some poems rime,
and some don't.

Contents

Foreword

I first met Sholom Roy Lavin (S.R. Lavin) in the summer of 2015 in Jensen Beach, when we were both living at Pitchford's RV Park. I detail our friendship in my in-progress spiritual memoir, a collection of connected essays entitled *Walking Prayer*. A few weeks ago, while cleaning my house, a small slip of paper drifted to the floor from a cabinet. On it, I discovered Sholom's handwriting. The note read, "Life is sweet gravy."

In "From the Book Called AMERICA" (the last poem printed in this memoir) Sholom writes, "I remember what my friend said...the last time I saw him, "Life is sweet gravy.""...A few days later he killed himself. He was dying of cancer and didn't want to suffer anymore...."

Reading *They Knew Me When* is like sitting with Sholom and listening to his stories. I got to hear many of them while sitting with him in my kitchen in the RV park. In this book, Sholom recounts poetry readings and profound statements about the human condition, braiding them with the poignant and beautiful story of the love and family he shared with his wife Rosemary, who died of breast cancer.

Any reader might hear echoes of their own lives within these pages. Poetry becomes resonant when it touches the universal. We begin with an idea, then narrow the focus to an image, an experience. The grief, the sorrow, the love shines through.

As Sholom writes in his afterword, "…poems also express the triumph and tragedy and suffering and beauty of our human experience, captured in the spoken moment of conception, transforming human experience into existential revelation."

Before Sholom passed away of his own illness, he asked me to store some of his belongings in my home. This accounts for the small slip of paper, the reminder, "Life is sweet gravy."

Sholom was sitting in my house the day I learned my brother, Miles, had killed himself in August of 2015. When I sobbed and fell to the floor, I heard Sholom in the other room, saying something to my partner at the time, telling him, "That's how I was when Rosemary died."

I rediscovered his note two weeks after my mother's colon cancer diagnosis. Sholom knew my mother. I introduced them. After Sholom's death, my mother took some of Sholom's old shirts—too worn and too fragile to donate—and she turned them into a beautiful wall-hanging, a quilt in which the breast pockets of his shirts serve as holders for his mementos, notes and pens. Two hooks hold the quilt on the wall in the guest bedroom. On one hook, we hung Sholom's old gray baseball cap.

The future is uncertain. As of this writing, my mother is facing chemotherapy treatments to shrink a grapefruit-sized tumor in her colon.

Sholom brought me into his life and shared with me his innermost fears, his worries, and his love for his late wife and their six children. Before he, himself, died of his illness, I promised him I'd publish his memoir.

As you read this book, try to imagine Sholom in the room with you. I hope you'll get to know this improbable poet a bit more through his writing. I often wish I could introduce people to Sholom, and now I can, through this book.

As Sholom said during his final days in hospice care—a poet until the very end—"The only choice was the universe or nothing at all."

Those are words I'll live by until the end of my own life, too. We love you, Sholom.

— Rosa Sophia Godshall,
poet and author of *Many Miles* (Harbor Editions)

Chapter One

To tell my story is to remember the era in which I came to know myself and discover the meaning of life. I'm recalling these times to offer a perspective on the decision I made to become a professional poet. I never wavered or looked back or had much time to regret the choices I made.

Between 1992 and 2007 I wrote four novels, a non-fiction study, *God's People in Search of a Destiny* (about the Twelve Tribes Communities), and saw *Voice in the Whirlwind* (Collected Poems 1978-2007) published.

Over a sustained forty-year span I was able to generate enough income to ransom myself for the express purpose of being free to write. My writing career can be appraised by the five hundred pages of published poems and the thousand pages of prose that are the concrete embodiment of what I had sought to accomplish. I created my own destiny and found meaning in what I voiced.

For the most part, I worked hard to get where I got. I didn't think the world owed me anything. I never wanted something else. I was satisfied with what I was able to accomplish. My father painted seascapes and played his banjo. He pondered the meaning of life. His "time" came and went. Finally, he was only whatever he could remember, and everything else was gone.

There are many stories of many people who "rest" in grassy yards, which tell very little about them. "Here lies Mildred" (one stone reads): "mother, sister, wife. 1914-1947."

Some died young. Very young. Some gave all they had to defeat Hitler. Many of them knew what "making do" really meant because they had endured the Great Depression. They were a generation of exuberant people who loved movies and dancing and hearty sandwiches and fast cars and milkshakes and expensive clothes. And, they made time to frolic on the beach. They built cities and ran businesses. Their legacy was formed in a history of what we now refer to as "the past." Looking back, one might also conclude that there was a measure of insanity that seemed "normal" (as Erich Fromm postulated) to those who were born into an insane world (when considering what happened in their time).

I chose the life of a career poet…a nebulous role… especially in America, where there is so much emphasis on material wealth. Writing poetry from a mentality of projecting a real alternative to "surviving" or being safe, or seeking economic success, meant living a focused life of complete engagement. I embraced a skeptical intellectual curiosity as a positive ideal, and I was willing to question the validity of most suppositions and accept the consequences of being "set free" from what I perceived to be an empty, lonely life founded on consumerism and conformity.

Poetry provided the doorway to a consciousness bigger than "self," a pure form of artistic expression, an existential commitment of soul and being, a vision of a higher purpose, a "higher self," cultivated to actively participate in a complete discovery process. I held fast to a progressive agenda within which language connotes complete meaning…physically, psychologically, emotionally, socially, and spiritually. Writing poems meant staking out a linguistic process of creating constructive word values.

For me, complete engagement was all about *commitment* and *discipline.* Study. Practice. Risk. Imaginative and experiential accomplishment. The written word. The spoken word. The substance of meaning seen and heard. An aesthetic determinism. A direction forward. I walked away from my planned career and risked all I had worked to establish on a vague hope that becoming a writer would validate my destiny. I would be "somebody."

Poetry, in its quintessential worth, expresses what human beings long for in our essence…the concrete connection back to Eternity, where Life makes sense because the spiritual nature of language reveals both mystery and meaning. Speaking is *élan vital* (the imperative and fundamental essence), as Pablo Neruda wrote, "Not to speak is to die."

My poems became the deeds that documented the process. In 1971, I quit my teaching job at the community college. I walked away from the security of a tenure-track career, which to that point in my life was what I had worked to achieve. I was twenty-six years old. I created circumstances which changed my life within a three-foot radius of where I was standing. I went to work being a self-employed full-time writer. I wasn't waiting for the world to change or waiting for a bus that would never come. Of course I wanted to be published. But my driving ambition was to have a product worthy of being published, and that was always forefront and never to be compromised.

My sensibilities were bent toward a notion of a common Humanity, intrinsically conditioned by a longing for social justice. I also retreated into an enveloping Nature as a way to find solipsistic peace. Like Pirandello's characters on the stage, I was in search of an essential meaning for my own life. I had been raised to be a pragmatist and a compulsive achiever. Self-examination and psycho-analysis were the fertile engines which propelled my escape from a humdrum existence. The substance of stripping away illusions and lies became subliminal themes that fueled my passion (i.e., my attitude) with the self-imposed motive to communicate worth and dignity to all people, regardless of their political views, or their financial status, or their job or profession.

I was in pursuit of an ideal self, a self-created self who sincerely believed that poetry gave voice to, and reflected, a common humanity, that poetry as an artistic form, asserts real and progressive human values. I saw myself as a creative dreamer with a democratic backbone. The nature of poetry was to expand one's being to discover and inspire "such stuff as dreams are made on."

The job of a poet as a professional expert was to evoke and establish a poetic language that spoke to what all people need: security, recognition, respect (i.e., esteem), and a sense that they are more than pawns in someone else's chess game. I was deeply rooted in being an American voice with a conscious determination intended to transcend finite experience, and I established within myself that what I wrote would have universal (or international) appeal.

Nationalism, racism, and fanaticism had produced the Holocaust. Ignorance and apathy had fueled the elemental breakdown of civilization, creating a murderous war machine without moral restraint. "The Manufacture of Evil" (from Lionel Tiger's title) was upon us.

Nothing greater shook the century than when the U.S. dropped the Atom Bomb and wiped out two entire cities of civilians from the earth in a matter of seconds. A pervasive industry was created with the sole purpose of building a nuclear arsenal capable of wiping out humankind.

No single event more stunned the world than the assassination of President John Kennedy. No idea changed our "world view" more than $e = mc2$. And then, there was the first picture ever taken of the Earth from outer space, a photograph that graphically revealed we Earthlings live on a tiny ball made mostly of water. Vividly, we knew the inexorable: we live in the black reaches of a nebular web, and our little planet is delicately wrapped with a thin covering of breathable gasses. If we did not already know or believe that we were all there is, that singular image of Earth revealed that we are essentially alone and, without dispute, a cosmic anomaly. Or, at the very least, we are not wrong to assume that we are all there is, the only beings in the universe who write books, crack jokes, make wars, and watch movies, get married or contemplate "the meaning of life." We are responsible for who we are and what we do.

My grandmother (my mother's mother), Ida, died in 1980 when she was 95. She had been born in the nineteenth century before invention produced the telephone, electric lights, cars, indoor plumbing, refrigeration, television, and radio. I was born in 1945, the year World War II ended, born with all the substantive conveniences and wonders that modernity and science had established. All the progress and comforts, scientific achievement and advanced technologies had also propelled humanity into the nightmare realities of the Nazi Holocaust (the blatant industrialization of mass murder) and the horrific obliteration of Hiroshima and Nagasaki (cities populated by non-combatants).

All my grandparents were immigrants and orthodox Jews. I was born on "Hungry Hill," in Springfield, Massachusetts. My grandfather, Israel, a fruit peddler, was a quiet, gentle man. My grandfather, David Lavin, was an earthy man who made his way selling blueberries and cattle. He was a "diamond in the rough." David was a sober realist with an inventive mind. He loved life, worked hard, and always told the truth. He shaped my boyhood with his indomitable command, his outspoken wisdom, and positive will. His wife, Rebecca, was the love of his life, and he lost his desire to live when she died. The Lavin family was a clan whose head was David. Under him, his three sons were raised and trained to work for the family's common good and economic interests. The family business prospered and expanded from 1950 to 1980. Rebecca died in 1956. David died in 1958.

When I was three years old, my grandfather Israel suffered a devastating heart attack and was rushed to a local hospital. He never regained consciousness. My mother took me in hand and went to the hospital to see him. We stood at his side and my mother wept. All around us the hospital staff of nuns were in a tizz, and I remember them scurrying to move as many patients as they could out onto the balconies.

I heard one of the nurses say, "He'll be here any moment." I stood with my nose against the rail and looked down into the courtyard. A limousine pulled in. The door swung open and a rather dapper figure of a man in a three-piece suit stepped out to the cheers and applause of patients and staff. He dropped to one knee and began to sing....

"Toot, toot, tootsie don't cry." Al Jolson was in town for a performance and was making the rounds, doing a number of free benefit appearances. His impact and staggering pizzazz captured my imagination. I didn't really know who he was, but I was immediately smitten. Life was bigger than I had ever conceived. Al Jolson was "bigger than life." Something grand had captured my attention. I was infected by the notion that there was a glorious aspect of being alive.

When I was four years old (1949), I saw a boy in an iron lung. He had contracted **polio**, which meant all his muscles were paralyzed by this incurable, often deadly, virus. It was believed that polio was a kind of "cold" that attacked a person's muscle and nerve fibers. America was gripped in an epidemic. No one knew what it was, how you prevented getting it, or what the cure could be. The country was mobilized to respond. In the movie theaters, during intermission, we were asked to give our pennies and dimes for the Jimmy Fund and the March of Dimes. In the ensuing years, until I was eleven years old, many people were stricken with polio. Everyone knew a victim because the disease had proliferated into every corner of society. Franklin D. Roosevelt (the President of the U.S.) had been paralyzed from it.

Characteristically, survivors often wore leg braces, unless their paralysis was so bad they had to be put into a breathing chamber called *an iron lung*. I was terrified of life. Maybe my dirty toothbrush had polio germs on it? Or, maybe you catch it from somebody at school…in the bathroom…*in the drinking water or from a dirty glass.*

Years later, plausible rumors suggested the entire epidemic had been manufactured by medical companies who had produced venomous batches of smallpox vaccine. I will leave that discussion to others who have done the research and can address this point with professional authority to do so.

The message embedded in my psyche was this: if the bomb doesn't incinerate you, then polio will get you. You could end up a helpless "vegetable" who couldn't even eat your food anymore or drink a glass of lemonade or even tie your own shoes. I lived in a perpetual state of hysterical fear…mostly unspoken, but never resolved.

Another episode of my early years was as traumatic as any one discovery could be. Between my grandparents' house and one of the public parks was the Shriners' Hospital, an institutional complex of buildings dedicated to the care of children. One building in particular was off-limits and shrouded in secrecy. (I'd actually been on the grounds of the hospital many times, but never had I ventured off a certain path that led to the park.) But my curiosity was unchecked, and I finally got up the gumption to sneak around the bushes and look into the window of the forbidden ward. What I saw devastated me. At first glance, I saw a boy with a head three times larger than his body. There were caregivers bustling about and each patient (child) had some visually shocking birth defect or hideously malformed body.

I was four years old. There was no way for me to assimilate or comprehend what I was seeing. I had ventured where I was not supposed to go, and I saw what was not supposed to be seen. My fear of real life amplified with no corresponding comprehension of what I had seen. Maybe I would look like that someday. Why did those children have to be like that? What was wrong with the world I lived in? I ran away and never went back. And I never told anyone what I had seen.

In 1952 (I was seven), we made a sudden, unscheduled trip from Maine by car to Springfield, Mass., an arduous four-hour ride. I was told nothing except there was an emergency and we had to go. When we arrived, we went directly to David and Rebecca's house. The family was gathered. David's sons were steeped in a secret council. My grandfather wasn't there but he was on his way home from the hospital. He'd gone in for minor surgery to relieve some pressure on a damaged nerve in his leg. Something had gone terribly wrong during surgery. His leg had been amputated. Even worse was that his leg had been removed above the knee, which meant he had to use crutches. There was a long period for rehabilitation, and ultimately he did wear an awkward prosthetic. But he had suffered an incalculable humiliation, and he was no longer a man of inner strength.

My grandfather David had been head of the family and business for more than thirty years. The Springfield Beef Company was becoming a major distributor in several states. The business was a grueling ordeal that required daily hands-on management.

Not only was David weak from surgery, he was mentally unprepared to surrender control of the company. Nor had he ever imagined a day would come when he would be sidelined so suddenly and absolutely.

When I saw my grandfather, he seemed broken and utterly at a loss as to what might be his fate. I could only be there as one of his offspring who loved him for who he was. He would always be a man deserving immoveable respect. And from that day to the end of his life, all I knew was that he was to be honored and heeded.

But his sons were quick to push him aside. The family business couldn't wait. David capitulated. A new generation of first generation Americans had come of age.

LIFE seemed unjust and downright dangerous, unpredictable, scary, and most likely, you end up in a tragic condition or dead. Embedded in my psyche was the notion that living an unscathed life seemed an unlikely possibility.

My father had his hip crushed in a freakish car accident when he was eight years old. By the time he was eleven he had been through seven or eight surgeries. The bone had infected. He had severe osteo-mellitus. The wound area was left open so as not to cause further infection. Leeches were applied to the affected area. Completely crippled and bedridden, he was sent home from Boston General Hospital to die. But my grandmother, Rebecca, had other ideas.

She put him on the roof in the sun, and fed him chicken soup. The infection dissipated. But the wound left a hole the size of a man's fist in his side. My father refused to accept his fate. He made up his mind to beat his debility. He would overcome, no matter what it took. He started by developing his upper body strength. He climbed the ropes and worked on the rings at the gym. He swam eight to ten miles a day. Like his heroes, Franklin Roosevelt and Jim Thorpe, he dedicated himself to hard work,

unrelenting perseverance, and an unwavering belief
that he would walk again.

At eighteen years old he had become a
formidable boxer, a swift and agile dancer in the
ring who packed a powerful one-two punch and a
deadly uppercut.

My mother was an ardent socialist and an
avowed atheist. My father was an avaricious seeker
who dreamed of being an artist (oils and acrylics).
They were first generation Americans who lived the
American dream (which meant they were consumed
by their desire to become successful and 'happy').
My father also swam every day, sometimes as much
as ten miles in fresh water lakes. As a consequence
of his experience and tenacity, I was trained to box,
to swim, and to be a resolute achiever. One simply
persisted until one overcame and succeeded.

My parents were also Depression kids who
believed that escaping from the ghetto depended on
getting a college education (neither of them had
achieved that goal but they had gone to high school
believing that a college education was tantamount to
real success in America). They were first generation
citizens. America was the land of opportunity, and,
with all its limitations, ours was a vibrant society.
And being educated was the way to advance and
find fulfillment. My father was a voracious reader.
So was my mother.

When I was five, my parents moved to Maine.
We lived on the coast. My father studied painting
with Nunzio Vienna, a somewhat renowned Italian
artist who was quite old but still working. We visited
him in his studio, which was a large barn filled with

his canvases including one striking life-size banner suspended from the ceiling of the well-known Da Vinci drawing of Vitruvian Man (1487 A.D.) spreading his limbs to touch an encompassing circle.

The years in Maine were serendipitous. Those times on the beach watching my father paint. We lived on Route 1, in a house once owned by a sea captain. In 1951, Wells was not much more than a rural sea town. But in the summer, there was an influx of tourists and vacationers. Just down the road, in the town of Ogunquit (an Algonquin word meaning "Beautiful Place by the Sea"), was a renowned summer theater headlining such stars as Maude Adams and Ethel Barrymore, and years later, Steve McQueen.

My father hired on a crew of lumberjacks to clear a few acres of woodland to make way for a potato crop. Their workhorses were stabled in our barn. I spent my free time hanging around the barn, enthralled by these magnificent creatures. Across the road and just up a ways was a boarding stable. I was determined to be around horses. So much so that the owner of the stables agreed to let me work for him as a stablehand raking out the stalls. He paid me twenty-five cents for each stall that I raked out. Within a year I was grooming racehorses and then trotting the ponies.

My love of horses, boats, and movies was intensified by a healthy imagination and a yearning for adventure. My father was also a voracious reader and thinker. He put Einstein's book *Out of My Life and Thought* in my hands and told me to consider what the smartest man who had ever lived had to say. He also encouraged me to read the novels of Howard Pease, Jules Verne, Edgar Rice Burroughs and Robert Lewis Stevenson. My mother's favorite book was *Studs Lonigan* by James T. Farrell, an epic saga of a young man's rise from poverty and common ethnic origins to become a successful player in the great American drama.

My father bought a turn-of-the-century encyclopedia. I read every volume twice. Volume "A" alone gave me exposure to Argentina, the Amazon, Attila the Hun, the atom, and James Audubon. My interest in ornithology was kindled and was to develop over a lifetime a fascination and curiosity that never waned.

In 1952, in the second grade, I scored 142 on the national IQ test. I was immediately transferred into the third grade class. I did not want to skip a grade. My friends and schoolmates were solidly formed. At that time I was an only child. I didn't particularly like my second grade teacher, but I really disliked the third grade teacher. So I rebelled. I refused to do my schoolwork or "perform" to please the adults who were pressuring me to follow the accelerated program laid out for me.

Two weeks later, I was sent back to my second grade slot. I got my way and stood up to the will of adult authority. I loved to learn, but I hated the regimen and disciplinary authority of grammarians. I was tagged as one who "does not work well with others."

My mother, concerned about my extrovert nature, wanted to direct my outgoing (and unchecked) behavior by studying dance as a way for me to express my budding showmanship, so she enrolled me in a school dancing class. I became a tap dancer. A professional dance teacher had been recruited by the school. She commuted from Portland twice a week and held dance classes in the high school auditorium. A recital of the best dancers was scheduled at the end of each term in the school auditorium for a Friday and Saturday night show. I was featured in two numbers.

For my solo, I was dressed as Aladdin in teal blue satin pants and shirt with a spangled white sash. I also performed a dance with a partner, a girl I was secretly sweet on. For that duet, I was dressed in a black suit and a bow tie. In my solo performance, I tapped up and down stairs with nimble agility. The dance teacher was in her early twenties, an athletic dancer with a professional resume. She was also quite pretty as well as vivacious. I worked tirelessly to learn what she knew and to meet her expectations of excellence.

The recital featured ballet, tap, singing, and acrobatic acts. Rehearsals for the show lasted for more than a week. A professional "MC" introduced each act. He was a locally recognized performer and a smooth-talking, handsome host.

My routines came later in the roster so I sat through every rehearsal from beginning to end. Then, without warning, at the dress rehearsal, we were told the MC had fallen ill and would not make the show. There was a scramble by those in charge to figure out how to overcome this setback. There was really only one solution, replace the man with someone who could do his part. The problem was he had an integral role. There was a complicated script with many nuances, jokes, anecdotes and lavish introductions for each of the acts.

Because my second dance number came near the end of the last part of the recital, I had learned all of the script for the entire show. I had memorized all the lines. I could recall every line. In the frenzy of the dress rehearsal, I was offered a chance to demonstrate my skill. Given the emergency, I was catapulted to audition for the job.

My showmanship was immediately revved up to meet the need of the moment. I was designated to be the MC and was given a black wool suit too big for me.

I was undaunted by my new role. When I opened the show I did an impromptu (if not obvious) parody of Ed Sullivan. The audience responded with wild approval. I was seven years old. I wasn't thinking much about being an actor or a sensation. My focus was completely honed in on my dance numbers. But the effect on me was apparent. I was the center of attention, the darling of the recital. And the audience loved me.

***

We were the only Jewish family in Wells. There was a deeply formed anti-Semitic mentality among the locals. Having been raised within the confines and protection of an all-Jewish community, I was then caste as an outsider and a miscreant. One incident that shook me deeply occurred when I was in the second grade. Several older boys smacked me around and roughed me up. They told me that I had killed Christ. I didn't even know what they were talking about.

My father explained it to me this way: Jesus was a Jew who had wanted the gentiles to become Jews. But they couldn't comprehend an unseen god. So they made Jesus their god and started a different religion. Judaism was premised on an unseen, unnamed power (or source). My father saw anthropomorphism as a weakness of mind and spirit. It was a topic of discussion between us for decades.

My third grade teacher made a comment that the reason Hitler had killed the Jews was because he was part-Jewish himself. And because he hated himself, he hated the Jews. When I came home from school and told my parents what the teacher had said, my father was outraged. We drove thirty miles to a reputable library and looked up Hitler's lineage. We did the research.

Hitler was a Protestant, fathered by a post office manager and a rather benign seamstress. Also of note, Adolph Shicklegruber (aka Hitler) was the child of an unwed couple (Alois Hitler and Maria Shicklegruber).

The next day, my father drove me to school and went into the classroom with me. He spoke openly in front of the entire class, stating categorically that Hitler was not a Jew. And then, as he left the room, he told the teacher to her face that she was an anti-Semite and if she were a man he would have punched her in the nose.

I was eight when my brother was born. That summer, my parents planned a trip from Maine to Connecticut to visit their friends and spend a week at the shore. Their plan was to leave me with my grandparents for a week, but they didn't tell me what they had in mind.

We arrived in Springfield at four in the morning and I was put to bed on the porch. I remember the sweetness of the cool night air, how weary I was from the long ride, and I slept knowing I was safe and in a place where I was loved.

When I woke up, I quickly realized my parents had not stayed and I had been left there without being told the situation. I loved my grandparents and being with them was not upsetting to me.

My grandmother, Rebecca, a small, delicate woman with a deep love of life, offered me breakfast. "What would you like me to make for you?"

"Nothing," I told her, emphatically. "I don't want anything." I mulled about in my irritation, wallowing in self-pity.

A short time later, she called me into the dining room where she had set out hot cereal, two fried eggs, toast, juice, and a full glass of milk. "What's all this?" I asked with as much bravado I could muster.

"This is your nothing," she said in her usual tone of kindness, with a dash of sweet irony. I was quite hungry and everything on the table looked delicious.

I stayed with them for ten days. I was reading Edgar Rice Burroughs's *Tarzan, The Ape Man*, and I fancied myself like an orphan who was raised in the jungle to love animals and protect them, who hated guns and killing, and who, having been raised by apes, found his identity in the natural world, free to swim, run through the woods (jungle), and answer to no one.

I also could not help but notice that my grandfather now slept in the guest bedroom while Rebecca remained in the bedroom they'd always shared. My grandfather had become sullen, pitiable, and "mad at the world." One of those nights, I crawled into bed with him and told him, "I love you, Grandpa. It doesn't matter to me that you lost your leg."

***

1959. I was fourteen. My father was thirty-nine. He worked at the family business seven days a week. Saturday was a shipping day, mostly spent getting sides of beef and other perishables to major retail markets. He left the house at four or five a.m. and would return in the late afternoon. Saturday was my day to play basketball. Friends, as well as local neighborhood rivals, showed up to form teams, and you had to show up early to get on a team. I was rushing out the door when my mother told me to take out the trash before I left. I told her I'd do it when I get home.

"Do it now," she insisted.

"No. I'll do it when I get home."

When I got home (at one p.m. or so) my father was waiting in the driveway for me. I knew right away I was in for it. He'd left work early.

"Son, your mother tells me she asked you to take out the trash this morning."

"I told her I'd do it when I got home."

"That isn't exactly right. You said no. Come with me." I followed him into the house.

In our basement, my father had a regulation boxing ring set up with all the accoutrements, including a punching bag, jumping ropes, and gloves of different weight and thickness.

"Put on your gloves," he commanded.

"But, Dad, I'm still in my street clothes."

"Just do it."

I chose the softest gloves I could and then I got in the ring.

"Put 'em up," he said.

"But, Dad…"

"Put 'em up!"

I did, sheepishly. My father took a quick side step and delivered a lightning jab into my gut. I went to my knees, winded and barely conscious.

Then he stood over me showing his gloved fist and spoke.

"You never say no to your mother. Never."

That was the last time I was reprimanded or disciplined as a teenager. You could say that was my last day as a child.

The family company, founded on a quality product, namely, our own brand of beef, had been selling about one hundred thousand pounds a week. A major client, a formidable ice cream company, was about to launch a new line to their menu, and our beef was selected for their burger. My uncles and father "designed" the contents of the hamburg meat.

We were catapulted from a successful company to a major distributor. We were "rich." We built new homes in the suburbs, and we joined a golf club. We took long vacations.

Oddly, in my own inner being, the wealthier we became, the less life made sense. What was our purpose beyond the glitz and the money? No one even asked. For my father's generation, there was no need to ask or know what else there might be.

As a loyal son, my part was to work hard, do what I was told, and support the family business.

When the big supermarket chains came along, we became their main supplier. 1959. 1960. The nation was locked in the civil rights crisis. In the south, we had seen hoses and dogs used against protesters. But up north, where discrimination was much more subtle, blacks were not served at soda shops or many restaurants. Our company employed Black men, some of whom had fought in World War II. The big food chains did not want "colored men" or negroes carrying the meat into their stores. Their customers were supposedly hesitant to buy meat touched by Blacks.

Our company was told by the stores to get rid of them, and use only white workers. My uncles and my father stood up to the storeowners and dug in on behalf of their Black employees. We did not fire our men nor would we change our delivery procedures. If big companies didn't want our beef because it had been touched by Black men, then they could go elsewhere.

We stood for civil rights. We stood for the dignity of our men, with them. It wasn't just about money and success after all. The Springfield Beef Company stood for fairness and justice, and equal rights. David's sons had not given in to the tyranny of prejudice.

I attended a college preparatory high school in Springfield, Massachusetts, a school with a significant Jewish population.

In 1960, there was a not-so-subtle anti-Semitic element embodied in society. Only white, protestant men became president. Jews were not welcome in certain restaurants nor allowed to buy homes in "restricted" neighborhoods.

One day, I was in line to get lunch with another Jewish student when an elitist gentile classmate said to his friend, "My people crossed the ocean to America on the Mayflower."

There was no doubt he meant it as a put-down, as if his lineage made him superior.

I responded to my friend in a loud affirmation, intended to be overheard:

"My people walked through the Red Sea with Moses."

Chapter Two

1963. I really didn't want to go to college, but my parents insisted. I was quite prepared to go into the family business and forget about getting an 'education'. I was cajoled by my father to go to college, and he agreed that I could work at the family business during summer vacations. I agreed only because my father would not have it otherwise.

The first week at school was devoted to an orientation program. As part of that schedule, I attended a convocation at which Norman Thomas spoke. At another session, I saw Sir Philip Burton recite soliloquies from Shakespeare's great plays. I sat in on a general introduction to Philosophy, and that opened my mind to the reality of being where I was, to learn about "the meaning of life."

For the next two years, I studied with T.H. Gaster (translator of the *Dead Sea Scrolls* and editor of Frazier's *The Golden Bough*). He was an ominous intellectual presence and a meticulous scholar who demanded intellectual integrity from his students, stating glibly to the class, "I speak to where your minds should be, not where they are."

Like most serious students in college, my focus was primarily directed to my academic regimen, and since I was selecting Philosophy and Literature courses, I spent most of my time reading the plays of Shakespeare or extensive selections from the Upanishads, the Vedanta, the Bible, Rabelais, Cervantes, Coleridge, Shelley, and Byron. I wasn't interested in politics or economics. I did attend Philharmonic Hall to hear symphonies composed by Mahler and Beethoven, and did see most of the great conductors of the age, such as Max Steiner, Leopold Stokowski, Sejii Ozawa, and Leonard Bernstein. For me, these were heroic figures whose personal auras seemed magical, charismatic, and I saw them as geniuses who stirred my love of great ideas through the forcefulness of their dynamic abilities to evoke the orchestra to convey the power of aesthetic euphoria.

I did attend a presentation by the newly elected Senator from Idaho, Frank Church (in 1963). Afterward, I was selected to meet him and be part of a photo op. He impressed me as a man of deep conviction who believed in a liberal reformation of America that would produce a more just society, an America that lived out its creed of equality and social justice. The encounter also reaffirmed my steadfast focus to remain a scholar and become a teacher.

Politics seemed shallow, intellectually stunting, a Quixotic pursuit to legislate rather than educate, and so, would not create deeply rooted change.

In 1965, I attended a "teach-in" meant to argue the pros and cons of the Vietnam War. It was a two-day event featuring Senator Bobby Kennedy. About fifty people attended and after the formal part of his talk, a few of us got to huddle around him. I could not help but blurt out the general dismay after President Kennedy's assassination. Did he believe Oswald to be the "lone gunman"?

In his own soft-spoken manner, he replied, "If I run for President and am elected, we'll have a new investigation and the truth will come out." And then he added, "But do not doubt there are guns between me and the White House."

***

I went with a college classmate to his audition for a part in *I Knock at the Door*, starring Alexander Scourby. He landed the part. The director (who later went on to direct *The Fantasticks* on Broadway) saw me in the audience and asked me to read for the boy lead. I agreed to do so on a whim and was immediately given the part. Three weeks of intense rehearsals and eleven performances followed. I did not want to be an actor, nor did I relish the harsh rigors of rehearsals.

When we took our breaks, however, Scourby dominated the off-time sessions with a brand of humor and joke-telling that ignited my intellect and love of comedy. He was a master of delivery, bravado, and awe-inducing focus. Scourby, known as "The Voice," is best remembered for his narration of the *Victory at Sea* and *The Bible*. His wife,

Lori March, also starred in the production. Our performances of Sean O'Casey's play earned critical praise and was well-received by packed audiences. I could have gone on to Broadway with a pre-approved ticket to a career as an actor. I was eighteen years old. Lowell Matson, the director, wanted me for the boy lead in *The Fantasticks*.

***

1966. I was twenty-one and attending a small liberal arts college in western Massachusetts. I was studying literature, philosophy and history, still intent on becoming a college professor. In the aftermath of John Kennedy's assassination, I wanted to fulfill President Kennedy's challenge to do something of significance, to be a useful and productive contributor to society.

In my junior year, I elected to study American literature with a very dynamic teacher, Anne Vliet. In those times, it was common to socialize with our professors, and so, when Anne invited me to visit her home, I was eager to do so. That's when I met her husband, R. G. Vliet, a prominently published writer. He impressed me as a fiercely dedicated artist with only one professional focus, to write.

My visits to their remote mountain hideaway were always for academic stimulation. I had neither a desire to write nor a propensity for being creative. But my talks with Russell were very blunt and insightful. I was astonished by his intellectual clarity and single-minded dedication to writing. He spoke of Hemmingway and Faulkner as if he were following in their footsteps. I was enthralled and swept up in the quest he had chosen for himself. His advice was clear and his discipline clearly established: *To write, to be a writer, and to produce writing that could be judged as culturally worthy.*

He told me that a writer must find his own voice and style, to be a one-of-a-kind artistic phenomenon, and to relentlessly pursue the craft of writing with no distractions or other endeavors. "Lock yourself in a room and write. Write one sentence a day, or one page a day…but write. Learn how to write. Read the great writers. Study the world around you. Learn the names of trees and flowers. And when you're ready, send your work out to magazines and publishers that pay for your work. That's the ultimate and only way to know that what you are doing is good enough to be considered legitimate."

It was as if he'd thrown down a gauntlet and challenged me at my core to rethink what I was doing with my life. But I never expected to take his advice. I wanted to teach and live a more conventional life. That's what I told myself. The idea of being a writer seemed too romantic, suitable only for the rugged geniuses and enormously talented, compulsive eccentrics. No, it wasn't for me. I would teach and be secure from the dubious quest to be recognized or appreciated as an author.

In Anne's class, I was reading Whitman and beginning to feel the stirrings in me that I was more than a scholar…but what? And to what end? Certainly not to become a writer. I took a long hike up Hamden Mountain, agitated but unconvinced. I was reminded of Wordsworth as he faced his solitude and oneness with Nature in the poem "Mt. Blanc."

Russell had stirred me and Anne had inspired me. The poets inspired me. Russell was a man of succinct personal conversation and not necessarily interested in impressing anyone with wit or ordinariness. He was fiercely focused on his work, on being a writer, on getting the work done. He embodied and exuded those qualities and character traits that proved he was who he claimed to be. He was genuine and steadfast.

My friendship with both he and his wife continued beyond my time in college. I visited them in Vermont (not far from Bennington) after some of my poetry was published. His advice and example had become part of my work ethic. I had learned how to work within the confines of my own boundaries as a writer and to use that foundation as the starting place from which to be creative and original.

Chapter Three

In the late 1940s, radio was the dominant source of home entertainment, and newspapers dominated public discussion. By 1950, television had captured center-stage as the marvel of a new age, a populist medium for communicating ideas, life style, and news. Real life was lived in austerity, affirmed by hard work and intelligent progress. TV resembled vaudeville as a delightful escape from the day-to-day real world.

In 1957, my parents drove two hours on a Sunday to visit their friends in Boston. The occasion—to see color TV. That evening, we watched the Dinah Shore Show. She appeared in an orange dress. The impact of the event went beyond me. TV was still the small box. Movies were big and grand, dramatic, scenic and powerful. Movies were "larger than life." TV reduced human experience to a vapid marketplace of shrunken and diminished possibilities. Expectations of a more progressive society were thwarted and controlled by a rigidly contrived, unimaginative programming of human thought.

By 1960, television was an all-pervasive cultural force that reached into every home, affecting people of all ages with news, drama, variety, and comedy, all the while weaving a narrative that the nation was connected by a documented reality, legitimized by the fact that you saw it on TV. What we saw reached into all our lives. The Kennedy-Nixon debates, Hal Holbrook's portrait of Mark Twain, and the Ed Sullivan Show represented the depth and breadth of what TV had become.

TV was no longer an escape from reality. We were privy to a séance of a national reality that had a real influence in creating the image of who we were and what we collectively believed because what we saw on television was reality. Perception supplanted reality. The pervasive nature of TV obscured the deeper human needs that weren't topics on air because those issues weren't marketable or easily visualized.

So much has been written about the assassination of John Kennedy that I can only echo what persistent researchers have stated. Mark Lane wrote more than one book on the subject (his *Rush to Judgment* is still the "bible" report on why we know Lee Harvey Oswald could not have acted alone and may well have been a "patsy").

Lane rehashed all the inconsistencies and misfitting pieces of "evidence" in yet another book, *A Citizen's Dissent*, in which Lane essentially repudiated the "theory" that a lone gunman took down the president. He went even further in *Oswald*

Innocent? A Lawyer's Brief. It's reasonable to assume the Warren Commission Report is riddled with lies and also misrepresents minutia for the purpose of obscuring the simple truth: that no one could fire a Mannlicher-Carcano bolt action rifle in the time required to get off four shots and have three bullets hit a receding, moving target more than a hundred yards away through the foliage of spreading trees.

No expert marksmen could duplicate or even approximate the scenario to any credible degree of accuracy. Watching the famous home movie of the shooting (the Zapruder film) anyone with eyes can see the president's head is blown apart from two directions, the first shot being fired from the front and hitting Kennedy in the neck and throat, whereas Oswald would have only been firing from the rear.

The significant detail to be raised here, for the sake of historical accuracy, is that the man accused of killing President Kennedy never entered a plea, never stood trial, and was never found guilty of any crime. Yet, he ignominiously wears the label as John Kennedy's assassin.

Moreover, Lee Harvey Oswald was murdered in a most bizarre shooting: he was gunned down on national television while in police custody in the Dallas police station. His autopsy was also spotted with misinformation, gross negligence, and scientific errors. In any case, all those records were "lost" or never written down in the first place. Lee Harvey Oswald may have actually been an innocent "fall guy" for a much broader and deeper conspiracy than any of us will ever know. Or, perhaps he was the best marksman ever trained to focus and fire a hand bolt-action Mannlicher–Carcano rifle. In one sense, it doesn't matter. The facts of the case have dissolved into historical surreality.

On November 22, 1963, all the lights on Times Square were turned off and a deep spiritual darkness fell over the American landscape. Times Square went dark and all Broadway plays were cancelled. Every television station suspended all programs and all the networks were broadcasting news and commentary regarding the president's murder *on a twenty-four hour schedule.* Or, when not offering news reports and commentary, the television stations simply showed an American flag at half-staff blowing in the wind, accompanied with mournful patriotic music.

Tragedy had bound our entire nation into a family experience. Shock, anger, disbelief, and hopelessness gripped a generation of Americans. The murder and "cover-up" of the president's assassination was fostered in a national experience of collective grief.

That undermining of the American justice system has never been assuaged or dealt with. A generation of Americans simply carried their grief with them for the ensuing decades. There was no closure, no resolution to the trauma. There was no "truth" to be known. The dream of a world without suffering and the idea that we, as Americans, were capable of creating a glorious future, was also put to death right then and there. A dark, cynical pessimism reached into the psyche of all who grappled with the enormity of John Kennedy's brutal murder.

From that was born a persistent distrust of all authority and law enforcement agencies. Implicated by innuendo in the "cover-up" were the C.I.A., the F.B.I., the Supreme Court, the new President (Lyndon Johnson), the broadcast media, and by association, anyone who accepted the notion that a lone gunman killed Kennedy. From that premise came the added belief that the entire Vietnam War was an outgrowth of a murderous regime that had usurped power by bloody coup and killed Kennedy because he was about to "end the war" being waged in southeast Asia.

Vietnam was the nightmare we couldn't wake up from. The U.S. policy wonks had it all wrong. South Vietnam was a Buddhist regime. North Vietnam was a Catholic culture. The U.S. government was bombing nuns and orphanages "back to the stone age." No one in the U.S. government understood that "Communism" to the North Vietnamese meant redistribution of wealth to create a society to feed, educate, and house "the have nots." It wasn't ideological. It was a social revolution. It wasn't Marxism for the masses; it was grass roots populism by the people seeking a real democratic government more like the way Americans had once struggled for, fought for, and died for.

U.S. government officials didn't take stock of the unjust wealth that the elite had accrued in South Vietnam either, mostly in the trafficking of opium (heroine) and other lucrative black market drugs. The Vietnamese people were not really engaged in a civil war. It was more about kicking the invaders and the foreigners out. They'd rid themselves of the French, and now the U.S. was the imperial oppressor.

The whole war was based on false assumptions, lies, criminal enterprise, and bad military decision-making. Endemic problems persisted. America was determined to win the war in Southeast Asia, adhering to policies that did not comprehend nor appreciate what the Vietnamese people were fighting for.

Kennedy ordered the Diem brothers to be "taken out." That caused South Vietnam to become destabilized. The next President, Lyndon Johnson, promoted a massive escalation of the war premised on an attack by North Vietnamese gun boats against the American fleet, an attack that had never happened and was fabricated so that Johnson could order a massive retaliation by sending in more troops. He bought into the romantic notion that the war was winnable. Johnson made it *his* war. And the war dragged on.

Nixon tried to "save face" by "not blinking." The plan or strategy (if you can call it that) was to "out-Korea" the Communists, which is to say, send as many men to a needless death as necessary to show the Chinese and the Russians that America would not back down, and our adversaries would know the U.S. had the will to win, no matter the cost.

As a consequence, an entire generation of Americans lost all respect for their own government, and came to realize that our country was being run by a totalitarian military-industrial complex. War was big business and "good" business. Or as one caustic comedian, Mort Saul, quipped, "It's a dirty little war, but don't complain, it's the only one we got."

Fifty-thousand Americans were sacrificed for the cause. How many more came home disabled or psychologically damaged or poisoned by deadly defoliating chemicals? How many came home maimed or spiritually demoralized? And how many Vietnamese died? How many villages populated by women and children and old folks were sacrificed in the name of the U.S. war god? It was a senseless war with no end in sight.

Chapter Four

In the 20th Century, progress and technological advances spurred on a Renaissance of artistic accomplishment. The continuum of intellectual revolution, human rights, and democratic literacy inspired a vibrant middle class to seek meaningful responses to enhance human development. Writers of enormous influence and intellectual depth were seen as powerful voices with substantive input. By the end of the century, the landscape was full of published treasures, but the onslaught of media and its mesmerizing illusions was, at the same time, reshaping values, mores, and standards of judgment.

Instant gratification and constant stimulation had engendered impersonal fulfillment, and was fragmenting consensus. While "the public" seemed sated, consumers were left substantively empty and still seeking the next "fix." Living from one high to the next with a hangover in between called "your life" had become a formula for a sublimated life-style of unrestrained consumption.

The social fabric of the 21ˢᵗ century has become a bizarre mix of alienation and isolation. Being absorbed into impersonal experiences, people hardly notice each other, even when together in crowds or mass gatherings (like rock concerts or in sport stadiums). The internet and the cell phone has created the illusion that we are more connected to each other, while, in fact, we are isolated more and more from each other without a cohesive cultural consciousness or an integrated world view.

In my early twenties (1965) I dared to wonder, "Is this all there is?" I wanted more than shallow experiences. I felt stultified. And it was clear to me what I was missing rather than me being provided with what I longed for.

I brazenly dared to ask, "Who am I, really?" or "What is life about anyway?" I wanted to know the answer to these questions. Most of my friends couldn't comprehend why I was so "obsessed" with such obtuse notions.

Technologies contributed to and established a paradigm that increasingly alienated people from one another, and all communication technologies became the unseemly replacements for real relationships, which were already obscured by intellectual stagnation. Our sense of humanity is dependent on the reality that we are connected as a society, a deeply integrating and deeply satisfying culture, so if not found in one thing, we find it in another thing (drugs, cars, mesmerizing music, sports, sex, etc.).

But this is for certain, rampant materialism is not motivated by altruistic tendencies or caring for others. Twenty-first Century life has devolved to be all about IT-SELF getting all *its* desires, or as Martin Buber might have adduced, "The self has all the IT one desires."

Martin Buber, iconic philosopher and best-selling author of *ICH und DU* (*I and YOU*) embraced life as spiritual being, wrapped in the mystery of an intrinsic power that cannot be explained nor dismissed. All attempts to verbalize or explain or define the essential mystery of life are limited to conceptual (or intellectual) abstraction. YOU transforms Being as God-consciousness when an individual realizes that Being is the direct connection when spoken with awareness of pure Being, or in the language of spiritual awareness, the élan vital. In contrast, all that is not alive is IT.

Literature in general, poetry more specifically, speaks to the infinite capacity of a human identity and consciousness to portray the visionary potency of the human perspective, to comprehend and embrace mystery, to evoke the power of an immortality that we long for as finite beings. For more than a thousand years, literature (and other forms of art) groped for and expanded the dimensions of human thought.

If one picture is like a thousand words then TV, projecting a thousand pictures per minute, changed the paradigm. Not only did TV stimulate us beyond our capacity to take it all in but also defined, by projection, ever more finitely what our minds and thoughts are directed to consider. In a matter of decades, the IT-World eclipsed the Living Word (YOU). Generations of human values and contested truth have been subjugated to known limitations. Finite definition usurped metaphor and mystery.

Media and technology has diminished our capacity to imagine the undefined unknown. Electronic transmissions and market-driven messages have altered our powers of perception. We have become the creatures of instant communication with no access to an alternative consciousness that contends with the totalitarian world view. The verbal-visualization of IT leaves nothing to the imagination and offers no alternative consciousness.

Poetry seeks beyond the known, an artistic expression meant to escape the bondage of the known. The power of poetry remains an uncontested and separate realm of human thought, emotion, and imagination. But within the confines of a society motivated by finite boundaries, there is little relevance or real impact left for art to either transform or challenge the IT-world for our latter-day existence.

For me, literature was the doorway to everything that television was not. The complexities and nuances of human thought, motive, the inner dimensions of the mind, and the imagination as a creative alternative to conformity of thought and to provoke the intelligent existential discussion that TV did not engage in nor care to. TV had become the medium of the lowest common denominator. Yes, there were intelligent exceptions, notably Rod Serling's "The Twilight Zone" and Roddenberry's "Star Trek." But otherwise, American TV was awash in cop shows and courtroom melodramas and glitzy game shows and sit-coms (with phony laugh tracks). A steady depiction of murder and violent behavior polluted the soul and mind of human aspirations. Literature was still a bastion of uncontaminated thought and continued to give voice to human values.

After receiving my Artium Magistrium in 1970, I became a more voracious reader than I had been during my years of formal study. My interests expanded to include biology, astrophysics, psychology, history, and philosophy. I read books by Gandhi, Martin Buber, Fritz Perls, Victor Frankel, Darwin, and I became enamored with a beautifully written masterpiece by Henry Beston, *The Outermost House*.

Through a professional friendship with Alicia Ostriker, I met her husband, Gerry, the man who "discovered" Black Holes. The excitement of the discussion about the origins of our universe, space, time, and the workings of nature all coalesced into my own creative impulses. I was drawn to the poets who were innovators as well as existentially honest in their formulations of thought. I embraced the terse brilliant minimalism of e. e. cummings, the iconic exuberance of Walt Whitman, the visionary capacity of William Blake, and the epic sweep of John Milton.

The opening monologue of "Star Trek" declared, "Space, the final frontier, to boldly go where no one has gone before." In essence, "Star Trek" was the best caricature of a comic book presentation of the deep unknowns that grip all of us. Who are we? How did we come to be? What is existence? What is life at its origin? Do we matter? Is there more to know than we are capable of knowing?

***

Anna Eleanor Roosevelt, author, mother, humanitarian, born into the wealthy Roosevelt family, married her second cousin, Franklin. She, the niece of Theodore, was a significant figure in my up-bringing. She belonged to a family of inherited wealth, who took seriously the notion that their privilege made them part of the "enlightened rich." She was an educated woman who held fast to the notion that her role in life was to bear the burden of her position to speak for those less fortunate. She dedicated her entire life to what she believed, and she lived to see her beliefs have a real impact on society and humanity.

She was First Lady from 1932 to 1945. She put all the prestige her position allowed to bring about civil rights and end segregation. She transformed government into a defender of the helpless. She loved humanity. She was sweet, kind, and caring. She worked tirelessly for social justice. She lived to see Civil Rights become the law of the land.

Her determination to see world peace become a reality caused her, after her husband's death, to single-handedly advocate for an organization dedicated to peace, and ultimately coerced the leaders of all the nations, when World War Two ended, to create the United Nations.

After weeks of meeting and negotiating, the leaders were prepared to go home and quibble some more about what kind of organization they should create. She embarrassed them, applied moral pressure, appealed to their better nature, and indicted their cowardly consciences, so that they dared not walk away without putting together some kind of world organization dedicated to peace, that would somehow work to prevent future slaughters and holocausts.

Finally, they all signed the United Nations Charter (1948).

In 1962, she drafted and wrote the thirty articles of the Declaration of Human Rights. She tirelessly waged a monumental campaign to see it adopted by the U.N. as a standard of law and decency for all humanity.

In that same time, my socio-political views were taking shape. The Civil Rights Era had spawned a new generation of civil disobedience against the blatant injustices of our society, and, simultaneously, spoke out against the war in Vietnam, a war that seemed to have no purpose, a war instigated by the notion that the United States had to stop the commies.

With a few students and professors I stood in a silent protest against the Vietnam War in the public square. There were less than ten of us. We were ridiculed, spat upon, and called traitors. Within a year there were fifty of us. Later, hundreds. Our nation was divided between the hawks and the doves.

Some of my friends had already fought in Nam, and they returned with stories of how the ground war involved murdering women and children, burning out entire villages, and torturing "enemy combatants." At home, as the anti-war movement was building, Lyndon Johnson announced that he would not seek another term as president.

I graduated from college and started working toward my Masters in Literature. I was accepted into a summer program to study at Oxford in England. While in London, I witnessed fifty-thousand people marching together against the War in Vietnam.

I left Oxford and spent time in London. I saw Donald Pleasance on stage in Harold Pinter's *Man in The Glass Booth*. I walked the streets. Spent time in gambling clubs. Then, I booked a flight back to the states. I flew home with a renewed sense of self. I made the decision to rededicate myself to scholarship and teaching. And to do what I could to protest America's unjust war in Southeast Asia.

***

In the Spring of 1968, Martin Luther King was assassinated in Memphis. Dr. King had gone there to support sanitation workers who were striking for higher wages. Then, within the month, his murder was followed by the assassination of Robert Kennedy, who had become the lightning rod for social justice and an end to the War in Vietnam. He was gunned down on the very night he had won the California primary for President.

Our country was thrust into the chaos of riots and social "revolution." Our nation was cast into the dark reaches of pandemonic disillusionment. The two most outspoken heroes of our age had been silenced, and there was only a sense of profound mourning. And we knew history had been altered forever.

In the summer of 1968, I spent a few weeks at my friend's summer cottage on a little lake in New Hampshire. We sailed, ate blueberry pancakes, and slept in the open air.

I wrote several poems. I didn't think much of them. If anything at all, they were academic contrivances that embraced "fiction-making" within stilted poetic forms. My friend, Bruce Chandler, liked the poems. But neither of us had much more to say about it until I got a call from Bruce saying that he had been invited by Harold McGrath to print at the Gehenna Press (in Northampton, Mass.) not far from where I was teaching.

Bruce had established a small fine arts press, The Heron Press. He suggested that I come down to Northampton, look over the situation, and consider making a book with him. Leonard Baskin had specifically given us carte blanche to work at any hours we wanted when Baskin wasn't printing. He gave us the keys so we could come and go at all hours. Sometimes we slept on the floor between our press runs.

When Harold had the time, he'd stand over Bruce's shoulder and encourage us to maintain the highest quality of what we printed. We were always made to feel welcome as well as acknowledged for the standards we maintained. We were young. We were serious. And we were being taken seriously.

I also had come to comprehend that my scholarship was less exciting than I had expected. I switched my field of specialty to modern literature. I took a job teaching high school English and hunkered down to complete my Masters at the same time. My thesis advisor, Hugh Ogden, was a somewhat prominent poet and became an influential friend. At the same time, I got my draft notice to report for active duty. The swirl of events made me consider fleeing to Canada, but I decided to resist induction instead. It was the first time in my life my beliefs and desires were to be put to a supreme test.

To a City Girl I Have Forgotten was published in the fall. We had printed 125 copies on Italian hand-made rag papers. Bruce presented six woodcuts with my nine poems. We collated and bound the books by hand. I took half of the edition and went to New York City to see if I could sell them. They were all sold in a matter of hours. I also had a significant (if small) but surprisingly favorable critical response to my poetry. I was invited to read at several prominent colleges and other venues.

In 1969, I took a slot teaching a summer course in World Literature at Greenfield Community College (in northern Massachusetts). I had given a poetry reading there right after Heron Press had published what was hailed as a beautifully presented letterpress fine arts limited edition. I had also received a number of very positive reviews of my poems, and the Dean of the college, having been impressed with me enough at my presentation (performance), offered me the opportunity to teach the course, which turned out to be a very exiting experimental program for high-risk students who had spent time in prison.

***

I rented a small cabin in Bernardston (about ten miles north), on the Vermont border. The cabin was nestled at the back edge of a pine grove, adjacent to a meadow where the landlord's horses grazed. It was a secluded sanctuary and pastoral setting. I was living out the reality of a modern day Thoreau. Like Henry Beston or Robert Frost, I had stepped away from the stresses of urban tempest nor longer willing to settle for the dull, twilight slumber of suburban comfort. I had also purchased a motorcycle that was built specifically to travel through the woods over rough terrain. I rode the fire trails north into Vermont and along the dirt roads that followed the rivers between remote towns and villages.

Several critical reviews of my poetry had suggested that I was a "neo-Romantic" poet. In as much as I believed what Byron had said, "Nature never disappoints," I suppose I did evoke elements of the neo-notion that one's experience creates the firmament for creative imagination, but I had also read Camus and Sartre. My own ontological comfort was forming to reflect that meaning and purpose were real only relative to what we say is real. My early poems were experimental more than declarations of any beliefs I might embrace. That search for meaning and the ultimate substance of my poems was the result of a lengthy and complex process of experimentation, cultivation, maturation, and organic development.

Bruce was inspired to want to make a second book with me, and I was becoming more encouraged by the small press phenomenon as a way to break into publishing and be taken seriously. But we could not foresee just how great an impact small press was to have in the ensuing decade. Our second collaboration, *A Ballad of the Cinema Kid*, was a more complex presentation of poems and woodcuts. Again, the edition sold out and established us in special collections libraries and among collectors of limited edition books. I gave poetry readings at five colleges in the ensuing season.

With my Masters in Literature accomplished, I pursued my career as a college teacher, landing a job at a community college teaching writing and literature. At the same time, I was embroiled in a bitter legal battle to resist the draft. I seriously considered leaving the country or going to jail. Essentially, I had to report for induction and then refuse to be sworn in. My determination to stand against an unjust war remained steadfast.

Mohammed Ali chose to go to prison rather than submit to the draft. No one who morally opposed the War in Vietnam was given the right to declare themselves a conscientious objector (except some religious sects). Ali was stripped of his heavyweight boxing title (unjustly) and he was prepared to receive a five-year prison sentence.

That summer I rode my motorcycle in the hinterlands and along the fire trails (dirt roads cut through the forests and only marginally maintained). One of my rides took me through the back roads between the most unpopulated countryside in Vermont and Massachusetts, on wagon trails that had never been paved, along the river to the town of Green River and then south to Colrain. This was a lost countryside of forgotten trails, remote farms, covered bridges and ancient native American archeological treasures.

The dirt road up from Colrain to Shelburne Falls brought me to Patton Hill, where a dozen or so "drop-outs" and "hippies" had established a commune. They were all transplants from New York City—college professors, a medical doctor, visual artists, non-conformists and "back to the land" activists. Among them, Larry Steinberg. He was a professor of anthropology, a gifted pianist and saxophonist. He also spoke fluent Spanish and was a voracious reader. We struck up an immediate conversation on a variety of substantive issues.

He introduced me to the writings of Carlos Castaneda, a colleague of Steinberg's, whose book *A Separate Reality* had become a best-selling, and provocative, analysis of an alternative consciousness induced by eating and smoking peyote, a cultural heritage embraced by the Yaqi (Indians). There was ample reason to believe that Castaneda's accounts were a unique blend of legitimate study and fictionalized narrative.

My focus linked these narratives to Blake's notion of the "doors of perception" as a root that

Aldous Huxley had also embraced, ultimately the same radical concepts that the counter-culture of the 1960s accepted. What causes a person to perceive the world with "new" eyes? What provokes us to change the paradigm? What gives us the power to make the choices that fulfill our existential destiny? These were serious questions being raised by reputable artists, New Age therapists, and brilliant writers.

Steinberg and I were both fierce competitors on the tennis court. Our chess games were tense, stirring, and adrenalizing. Our discussions never lacked for pondering the great mysteries. We spoke about how life forms evolved, how cultures arose and civilizations fell.

On one occasion we challenged each other to tell jokes the other had never heard. We agreed to end the session after a three-hour ordeal of non-stop repartee.

We sailed in Massachusetts Bay. We climbed mountains.

Our friendship continued over a forty-year expanse. In the late 1980s, after a decade of teaching, he left academia and went to work as a social worker. In his mid-forties he embarked on a career in the movie industry, working as a gaffer, a grip, a construction carpenter, and ultimately, a camera man. He worked for Spike Lee constructing the set designed for *Malcolm X*, his camera team won an Academy Award for *After Midnight*, and he worked camera one for Paul McCartney's concert at Yankee Stadium.

As the years passed, he also became an important reader of my writing, a critical voice I could count on to be both intelligent and honest. His sudden death in 2008 was shocking and cataclysmic. He suffered a massive heart attack while riding his bicycle in Manhattan. He collapsed and never regained consciousness.

1969. As a locally known poet I was invited to a poetry reading and a guest luncheon with Jon Silkin, an English poet. I was bowled over by his commanding presence, his audacious outspoken manner, and the fluidity of his writing and reading style. I was introduced to him and we got to speaking. I told him about my draft resistance. Without hesitation, he offered me sanctuary in Northumberland (where he made his home). After the event, I offered to give him a ride to the train station, but the train had already left and there was a moment of decision before him. I offered him a bed in my apartment and a ride to where he had to get transportation the next morning. He accepted my invitation.

We spoke of many poets, of literature, of current events, and of being Jews. Jon was a fervent Jew, not in any religious sense. His was an individuality bound up in a cultural and historical identity. In January, I bought a ticket to Edinburg, quit my teaching job, and took up residence in Jon's house. He was a true mentor and guiding intellect. Jon had relocated from London to Newcastle-upon-Tyne and had established *STAND Magazine*, a quarterly featuring poetry, fiction, and literary criticism. Internationally recognized for its editorial prowess and durability, the magazine had become a significant and respected publication. Each issue found its way to libraries and subscribers. And then, uniquely, Jon loaded up his mini-van and drove through England selling the magazine door to door in cities like Leeds, Liverpool, and at a number of "red-brick" colleges.

Jon saw himself as a working-class socialist, and he fervently believed that a poet ought to be paid for their work. *STAND* paid its contributors. He had also cultivated a scene of Northumberland poets who were actively giving readings, publishing, and enjoying each other's success.

I worked with Jon and his wife Lorna as an assistant: We read submissions, we packed up envelopes, and mailed out the magazine. And I accompanied Jon on several selling forays. He also furthered my development as a writer by encouraging me to read the poets who had shaped the modern era. I asked Jon if he wanted me to pay rent or in some other fashion repay him for his generosity.

He told me that someday, someone would knock on my door as I had knocked on his: "Remember how you were received. You do the same."

Those weeks and months I spent with Jon spawned a different quality and depth of writing from what I had processed and observed. My writing became more political, more confrontative, provocative, and more emphatically metaphoric. I returned to the United States with a stronger sense of self and determination.

Those poems became the body of work published in *The Stonecutters at War With the Cliff Dwellers* (1971).

Bruce asked me to come along and be part of a crew to help Jim Cooney move his printing press, a rather large Kelly B, off a pick-up truck and into Cooney's shop at Morning Star Farm. Among those there to help was Gregory Gillespie. There was an air of camaraderie among us and our conversations revealed that we shared sympathies to be sure. All of us loathed the war in Vietnam. We also understood the depth of social injustice that persisted in our country, and we saw the uprising of prisoners at Attica as proof that Black men were being systematically targeted and sent to prison for long sentences (usually on drug-related offences). A pattern of racial injustice wasn't hard to see.

On one occasion, in 1971, Cooney, Chandler, Gillespie, and I had traveled together to Greenfield to support a local artist who'd been arrested for selling pornography. His drawings and paintings were in the genre of Classical and Renaissance motifs. When the judge came into the courtroom, we heard the bailiff say, "All rise."

Cooney wouldn't stand up or take off his barrette. The judge threatened him with contempt. Cooney said he'd take off his hat if the judge would take off his robe, and he'd stand if the judge came down off his high seat. Gillespie and Chandler and myself literally dragged Jim out of the courtroom spitting and fuming. We were just trying to keep him out of jail. The artist was found guilty and only later was that verdict overturned by a higher court.

Gregory and his wife Fran and their two children lived only a few streets away from where Bruce and I had set up shop in Williamsburg. They were both brilliant and prolific painters. My friendship with them extended beyond a professional association. We shared a social life, we were engaged in a constant dialogue about art, and of course, there was always the political ramifications from our national nightmare to hash out.

Greg and I enjoyed sparring over artistic standards and ideas. We were friends for thirty years. I spent many hours with him in his studio. On two separate occasions he allowed me to "contribute" to his projects. I wrote the word "electricity" on a yellow blotch in one of his 4' x 8' murals and then, many years later, at his studio in Belchertown, I sat on a wooden chair in the wet paint and left a distinct impression. We were iconoclasts, anti-establishment and non-conformists. We were good friends who respected each other's work.

During his last years, Gillespie had been battling leukemia. He had endured painful bone marrow transfusions. I saw him for the last time when I stayed the night at his place only days before he took his own life. He told me that the transfusions had failed and the doctors were suggesting a radical, experimental treatment that was both dangerous and painful. They also wanted fifty thousand dollars to administer the drug. He told me that whatever he had left was going to his children, not the doctors. And he also made it very clear he was tired of the suffering he'd experienced.

In 2010, I stood before his life-size self-portrait in the National Gallery in D.C. It was as if my friend and colleague had found his final resting place, as centerpiece in the gallery, a powerfully clear rendition of his stern attention to reality and a testimony to his spoken visualization, "Life is sweet gravy."

***

1971. I was scheduled to give a poetry reading at a local college in Springfield, Mass. The event was sponsored by the English Department, and they'd promoted my reading in a significant way. I invited my grandmother and my father to come. My father had to take time out of his busy work schedule to be there, so in order to facilitate his coming, I planned to meet him at a gated entrance where school officials had reserved parking slots. When I arrived at the parking lot, my father had already put his car in a VIP parking place.

"See, son, that's why I drive a gold Cadillac. What I want to know is why you are throwing your life away writing…ditties."

My grandmother Ida also attended my reading with my mother, after which Ida came up to me as I was leaving the stage and said, "Shlomo, I didn't understand one thing you said, but you looked…beautiful."

1970. Bruce Chandler and I drove through and canvassed a chunk of western and central Mass. looking for a suitable set-up for us to establish a letterpress shop which would also have accommodations for us to live on-site, have working studios, and share our creative collaborations every day. There was an ominous sense of destiny for us as we drove through the hills around Amherst during a total eclipse of the sun.

We ultimately came upon an old general store in Williamsburg, at the corner of Buttonshop Road and North Main Street. Our first major project from that location was to be our third collaborative effort, again, nine poems and six woodcuts. The plan was to strike the book on an antique Washington Press.

So we went to work setting the poems I had written either in Bernardston or in England when I'd been staying with Jon Silkin. I selected the poems and Bruce made sketches for cutting images in wood that would in some way reflect the content or nuance of particular poems. At that same time, when we were designing our book, the Beatles released *The White Album*, a double LP, on their own label, Apple Records. That album was commercially successful in a way that redefined their popularity. It was also an expensive album.

I suggested to Bruce that we make a similar "statement" and produce a book that was strikingly set apart for both its presentation as well as its content. We decided to move the production of the book to the Gehenna Press, where *The Stonecutters* was actually printed, on Baskin's Kelly A. Our book was 18" by 24," and it was our most expensive book to date. The regular linen over boards copies were twenty dollars each and the deluxe, boxed, "head copies," printed on hand-made rag papers, were fifty dollars each.

Once again, Bruce presented six woodcuts with my nine poems. The book was printed at the Gehenna Press with the help of Harold McGrath and Danny Keleher. We contracted a most prestigious bookbinder, Arno Werner, to box the head copies, and his apprentice, Grey Parrot worked on the hard-bound edition. I worked with Arno at his studio in Pittsfield as well. The book was received among collectors and libraries with much acclaim.

The printing and publication of *The Stonecutters at War With the Cliff Dwellers* by Heron Press instigated a somewhat impressed librarian at Clark University in Worcester, Mass. to arrange for my appointment as poet-in-residence for the January Term, 1972. Clark University had become a flamboyant, avant-garde "hippie" school (and scene) with a profoundly intelligent and talented student body. There was a bedlam of marijuana and LSD prominently in use, but the romantic hey-day of those drugs was climaxing, and Massachusetts had become *de facto* decriminalized. Or, at the very least, no one wanted to make a big issue out of the drug use (quite openly evident at that time).

In the post-era of Woodstock, it was a time of experimentation, redefining of goals, realignments of social norms, and changing political landscapes— a time of discovery.

I packed up my 1968 black Volvo sedan (with

my tea pot and a tin of Darjeeling) and drove from Williamsburg, Massachusetts to Worcester along scenic Rt. 9 (heading east). The countryside between Belchertown and the Brookfields was especially beautiful, and having been enamored with Hardwick (Mass.) and Barre, I began to search in that area for a remote and exotic setting in which to settle.

I stumbled upon an old farmhouse, nearly in ruin, on a remote dirt road in West Hardwick, almost abutting the Quabbin Reservoir. It had been a 50-acre farm of meadows and forests, with two hard-water wells, an old barn (collapsing), and a harness shed (also dilapidated).

For some time I had been considering the notion of being part of a community of artists, whose aim was to work and produce art—an artists' colony with professional poets and writers having cabins spread throughout the property, with the main house available for common use. The years I had spent working with Chandler at Heron Press in Williamsburg had also been a time to cultivate many sincere friendships with other artists, but there was no consortium or enveloping environment to stimulate creativity. That vision was always illusive and never quite came to fruition. But, in its place evolved a real-life community that existed from 1972-1974 in its initial phase, then in a more eclectic version, from 1975-78, and finally, voted by its members to be dissolved (1980).

S. R. Lavin

1972. October. I moved into the farmhouse, which looked east to Dougal Mountain, after putting every dollar I had into the down payment (with no money left to meet even the first mortgage payment). I withdrew my retirement funds from three years of teaching in the public schools of Massachusetts, which gave me a few months to scramble and devise a plan to get a community started. At that time, the vision was to operate a small letterpress shop and produce books of poetry.

The Four Zoas Press printed poetry chapbooks in limited editions. Simultaneously, the press published *The Four Zoas Journal of Poetry & Letters*, a voice of dissent against WAR, and against the Vietnam War in particular. The first journal was issued in 1974 and evoked the spirit of conciliation to all sides, declaring: AMNESTY.

In the years prior, I had spent quite a bit of time with Bruce Chandler, working with him as his partner in the Heron Press (as the poetry editor and distributor-salesperson). Both of us had been given a significant access to the Gehenna Press (Leonard Baskin's shop), and then, from there, we set up our own shop in "Burgy."

Those years were fruitful and productive. In 1973, we published our anti-war pamphlet *Cambodian Spring*, nine poems and a rather shocking front piece by Chandler, a grinning skull of death declaring the horrors of war, the horrors we had come to know in Vietnam in particular.

"Confucian fuck-ode welcomes you the chamber of horrors.

The blind are lead to supper, confessing their

crimes to the wind." (*Cambodian Spring*, Heron Press, 1973.)

Those poems were especially significant because one of my mentors, George Oppen, had enthusiastically endorsed them and Jon Silkin had published some of them in *STAND Magazine*. Later, I recited the entire booklet of nine poems for an audio version, orchestrated with an innovative new-age electronic musical score by H. Norris. That was soon published by *Black Box*, an Audio Poetry Magazine (Washington, D.C., 1975). The entire sequence of twenty-five poems later appeared in my collected poems, *Let Myself Shine* (Kulchur Press, 1979).

Bruce and I spent many hours playing chess with Cooney, and sometimes working on our letterpress books out of Jim's shop. (Cooney's publication was *The Phoenix*.) When Heron Press moved back to Boston, and I transitioned to Hardwick, our printer, Danny Keleher, went to work for Jim. I bought the Kelly B (letterpress) from Cooney, which at one time had been owned by Harry Duncan at the Cummington Press.

Jimmy also sold me a small platen press that had previously been used by Anaïs Nin. The "small press" coterie of poets and printers was almost a family of long-standing fame among a certain underground society of avant-garde dissidents and literary innovators. Henry Miller had also been an early contributor-editor to *The Phoenix*. Cooney had come out of the Black Mountain poets, a "school" of radical, free-thinking writers, war resisters, and social experimentalists.

I had also become a good friend and protégé of Jon Silkin (the founding editor of *STAND Magazine*). I lived in Jon's house in Newcastle-upon-Tyne, in England (1970), and there, as an editor apprentice, I learned from Jon how to market inexpensive poetry books to ordinary lay-people as well as to students at colleges. Jon was a working class poet (and a socialist) who believed in an honest wage for honest work, and with that standard, he established the policy that working poets deserved a working wage. *STAND* paid writers for their poems, usually five to twenty-five dollars per poem, and a little more for fiction and essays.

Scrambling to make mortgage payments and meet other economic pressures during those first few months in West Hardwick, I sold the barn to a neighbor. I sold the wide boards and some of the hand-hewn beams for enough cash to cover two payments on the mortgage. Then, I placed a one-time ad in the New York Times Classifieds, offering the farmhouse and 18 acres to any purchaser interested in having a communal residence there. The selling price: $24,000.00 (the amount of the mortgage). That would leave me 32 acres that I would own outright, mostly comprised of forest with one high meadow (on the other side of the dirt road from the farmhouse). My scheme was for that land to become the stead for an artists' colony where cabins could be built and summer-time visitors would be welcome to stay for short periods, make a contribution in labor, do their art, and be part of a dynamic environment.

Chapter Five

While at Clark University, I taught a poetry class and had become intimately involved with a musical band of renegade students who emulated The Grateful Dead. But they also had a very unique creative pulse of their own. They called themselves Cat's Cradle, in homage to Kurt Vonnegut's novel. One of my students, Dan Carr, invited me to write a song with him for the group. Later that year, Dan and I gave our first poetry reading together with other media artists, combining our poetry with a psychedelic light show. The concert included two sets by Cat's Cradle.

And so, from that gig at Clark University, we were already forming a cohesive union of working artists, and it was at that event we introduced our first song, "Calling to the Waters" (published by the Peer Group, 1975). The song eventually became a kind of a poetic theme for us. The band was invited to work in a state-of-the art studio in New York City, where we recorded several of our songs through the Peer Corporation.

At that first evening performance at Clark

University, we invited people to join "The Horde." The evening was moderately successful (about a hundred were in the audience) and that led to many paying gigs over the next few years at colleges, cafés, and in concert halls. Our run heroically culminated in our appearance at the Five Spot in New York City in 1975.

From the get-go, in 1972, there was an excitement about what we were doing at the farm. Karen Fisher brought her pottery wheel to the farm. Michael Gonnick (aka Guru Ganesha) and I wrote "Valhalla Country Club" (published by the Peer Group, 1974), a farcical thigh-slapping new age mountain-song, with a foreboding ending verse that confronted the abject choice between nihilistic notions and existential reality.

We composed that song sitting on the porch at the West Hardwick farmhouse on a sunny afternoon during Indian summer in 1972, with a warm sun in our face and the bees buzzing in our ears. That year, from fall 1972 to spring 1973, was a renaissance of creative people passing through the region, and among them, the ones who stayed and then formed the initial community.

Not much later, we dubbed our land The Four Zoas Farm, which was about 20 miles east of Amherst, Mass. Poets, musicians, new-age rogues, ex-Vietnam vets, hippies, nature freaks, herbalists, potters, intellectual heretics, pot farmers, book-makers, printers banded and bonded together to begin work on the communal property. Mostly, during that first vibrant summer, we all lived in tents and used the farmhouse for a common place to socially gather. We also planted a rather large community garden.

But later that first year, I sold the farmhouse with 18 acres, and we all moved across the street and started to build The Eating House, our first major project, in the high meadow.

We also converted a swamp into a lovely freshwater swimming hole. And, as that first summer came to a close, we put on our first poetry festival, with some fairly prominent, as well as obscure, poets reading from their works. And of course, the Cat's Cradle Band performed as well. The number of guests and listeners (about 200 people) was actually quite staggering to me. More people turned up than had at many other events or venues I'd performed at, many more than had come to other readings at fairly distinguished universities, galleries, and poetry scenes.

We had also grown a rather large garden of food that first year. The harvest was impressive. In the autumn, some moved on. Some went back to school with the intent of returning in the spring, planning to pick up where we had left off. The Eating House was still under construction.

Among the poets who visited the farm and read at various festivals were Diane Stevenson, Mark Weiss, Morgan Gibson, Ken Smith, Bill Tremblay, Mac Wellman, Gerard Malanga, Julie Sheinman, and Dan Carr.

Among the musicians were John Tuttle, a kind of set apart musical genius, and the regulars from Cat's Cradle: Harry Norris, Michael Gonnick, and Bryan Depesa.

In that first year, Tom and Diane Dunigan also pitched in and joined us. They lived about five miles away, in a cabin in West Brookfield, but they spent nearly every day on the land. We embarked on a new kind of learning experience, though we hardly knew what to expect or what the goal was, if any.

Essentially, we were against the war and against "the system." And we had come to understand that being "against" what we loathed wasn't enough. We needed to find out what we were "for." It wasn't enough to be against the "establishment." We needed to establish something ourselves. If only for ourselves, we desired to be credible examples of *something*. But what? We were in search of ourselves. Our identity as Americans, boomers, artists, and worthwhile human beings was all at once at stake. We knew we either had to "put up" or "shut up."

Tom was an intuitive man, salted with common sense, and he became a true friend. He'd been a football player and a refugee from an upstate New York traditional middle-class life. But a near fatal car crash in 1972 left him with only one leg, and he was reeling from the devastation. I was hitchhiking on Route 9 when we met. He picked me up and gave me a ride to the farm. I was pretty scared when I saw him driving the car without using his one leg (it was still in a cast). He used his cane to push the accelerator pedal and the brake.

We smoked some marijuana together, and I explained the vision for the farm. The very next day he brought his family over. We were good friends ever after. Tom built a log cabin in the woods in the third year of our communal "experiment." Soon after that, Tom went back to school and became a registered nurse, then a chiropractor, and then went on to become a teacher. About five years after that initial encounter, he moved away to Pennsylvania and built a home for his family on a sweet little piece of land near the Delaware Water Gap. Tom was an "earthy man." He loved to get down in the dirt and grow food. He also introduced goats to our conclave, and we all got our start drinking goat's milk.

He was a friend of Ben Harris, a rather well-known herbalist who had a radio and TV show which was broadcast from Worcester, about 30 miles away. Ben made frequent trips to the farm to take us out on nature walks, and we also went on air with him a few times. The Watergate Trials and the nagging "winding down" of the Vietnam War were like an ever-present reminder to us that, in our time, we were witnesses to the staggering fall of America as we had once known it. We were seeing a president about to be removed from office. And, we were seeing our country embroiled in a never-ending undeclared war, and it was the first war America might lose.

The Four Zoas Farm was a short-lived phenomenon, at its apex of activity in the summer of 1973 through the summer of 1975, when Nixon resigned. During that time, and then over the next five years, the Four Zoas Press published fifty or so poetry chapbooks, nine issues of the *Four Zoas Journal*, as well as several "broadsheets" (individual poems for framing) by Jon Silkin, George Oppen, and Gerard Malanga. The letterpress was established in the old tack house on the farm, and through those times, we owned and operated five antique letterpresses.

Beyond the poetry, pottery, and the vegetables and cabins we built, we engendered an outlaw mentality founded upon our belief that the Vietnam War was immoral and wrong. Yes, we were pot smokers, but what bound us together was our rogue belief that "the system" was already too corrupt to be salvaged, and we were going back to the land to find a different way to live. Our little group (ten full-timers and forty or so drifters) had "pierced the veil of modernity" to reveal a monstrous corporate villain, an energy glutton, perpetuating an unjust society, polluting the water without seeming care, spraying pesticides, and poisoning the food supply, touting "nuclear" medicine and unsafe powerplants that were stock-piling radioactive waste. With a growing population of cancer victims in epidemic numbers, we turned our attention to learn about healing herbs and alternative medicine.

We saw a society that was tyrannically racist, suppressing Black Americans, marginalizing people of color, condemning the poor, disrespecting old people, gunning down students protesting the war, and drafting an unwilling population of young men who were forced to squander their lives as "cannon fodder" in order that an unjust government could fight an unjust war. It was "us" against "them," the hawks and the doves. And the war dragged on.

We wanted to get off the grid, so to speak. We wanted to eat organic foods. We studied alternative therapies. We established food co-ops. We baked our own bread. We ate brown rice. We studied books like *Back to Eden* and *Foxfire*, *White Sugar Blues* and *How to Live Sanely and Simply in a Troubled World* to help us live a more wholesome, healthier, and happier existence. We focused on our friendships. We were willing to be builders with our own hands, and we weren't afraid to work hard and long by the sweat of our brows. It was more than just a time for learning and more than just an experiment in alternative living.

We fully expected "the system" to collapse and leave behind a ruined civilization. So, we saw ourselves as preparing for a real life that would emerge from what we were building. We hardly knew who we were or who we were becoming, but we were clearly at the end of one era and at the beginning of another. We were for peace, and we wanted healthy change in ourselves and in the socio-political fabric of America. We became farmers, house builders, teachers, nurses, chiropractors, and parents. Along the way, we challenged ourselves to be better human beings.

By 1972, most people realized that the government and the "military-industrial complex" was hell-bent on its own course, regardless of public opinion or sane decision-making. And it wasn't just in Vietnam we could see the effects of their errant policy. We saw the same oppressive mentality support brutal dictatorships in Argentina and Chile, in Mexico, and we witnessed the storm trooper mentality at work in squelching the riots in America. We saw the bare teeth of the monster at Kent State where students protesting the war were gunned down.

In the aftermath of the late 1960s, when war protests and new age ideas had produced a "counter culture"—with distinct music, diet, clothing, and new allegiances based on a belief that Vietnam was wrong—all the cards were on the table, face up! The lines had been drawn. The hardhats on one side, the longhairs on the other. McGovern vs. Nixon. Good vs. Evil. War vs. Peace. Oppression vs. Justice. The assassination of Robert Kennedy and Martin Luther King, Malcolm X (and later John Lennon) had left an indelible impression on us all:

Watch out...because if you sing too loud or speak the truth and get heard, instant karma will get you.

We had the uncomfortable feeling what it must have been like for German citizens during World War II, those who saw Hitler as an evil and immoral man, those who hated what their government was doing, but were powerless to change it. And the war dragged on.

Fifty-thousand American men slaughtered.

How many Vietnamese? How many maimed or bombed into homelessness? And the war dragged on. So, we went back to the land. It was really a spiritual journey as much as physical attempt to purge ourselves of the national guilt.

Yes, we had our own militant mind, to oppose evil by speaking out, protesting, and being blatant in our disrespect for those in authority. In the tradition of Thomas Paine, we published anti-war literature. We were dissenters, iconoclasts, and muckrakers as well as middle class refugees with talent, gumption, education, money (though not so much as we needed) and we believed we had stumbled upon a new set of truths that would take us to a new way of living.

We dreamed of solar power and economic justice (redistribution of the wealth) and a clean environment where our children would live in a better (more just) world than the one we saw all around us. History demonstrates (by revelation and facts) that American intervention in other people's countries for their own good is not morally sustainable. And to that end, the sacrifice of American men and women is neither justified nor acceptable. The brutal destruction of someone else's homeland as a way to save them from what Americans believe to be their horrible lives, is not justifiable. The deaths of hundreds of thousands of innocent civilians is not justifiable. It's not "good," and it's not "just," and it's not necessary!

The Vietnam War exposed the insanity of the U.S. government's policy, which was devoid of a moral purpose or even a sound military objective. But on the ground, in the bush, and in the daily prosecution of the war, only one glaring reality remained. Thousands of American troops were dead, wounded, and spiritually damaged. A national trauma unfolded, created political upheaval in the states, and exposed the illusion that any good could come from the utter waste of resources, will, and patriotic loyalty.

Over the course of the war, and then for years after, I spoke with many returning soldiers. What they had experienced, or endured, and what they could not justify within themselves haunted us all.

One man was diagnosed as "mentally unstable" because he would not stop talking about the inhumanity of the violent treatment of Vietnamese villagers. A helicopter pilot told me about running drugs for his superiors.

The most devastating testimony came from a man who had become a headmaster at a private high school. While in Vietnam, he had been an officer leading a platoon down a country road when a young boy ran toward his men waving something in his hand and calling out to them. As dictated by normal procedure, he "wasted" the boy. With a burst from his M16, he cut the boy in half.

The boy had a chocolate wrapper in his hand, hoping to beg some candy from the Americans. The 2nd Lieutenant threw his rifle to the ground and vowed never to carry a weapon again. He was ordered to pick up his rifle or face court martial. He refused. In fact, he asked to be court-martialed. Instead, he was shipped home and quietly discharged. As he related the story to me, he began to weep bitterly.

I held him in my arms. "How do I live with what I did?" he whispered. "I killed God."

***

Our efforts on the land—and our work as writers and artists—was framed by our stance and status as war resisters. The anti-war movement, at one time, had been the driving motivation for a new configuration of young people (in the U.S. and around the globe) to "drop out" and confront the steamroller of totalitarianism before the whole world was just "a giant prison mess hall on a skimpy budget," to quote Mark Weiss. Of course, we were naïve. Yes, we were idealists with very little principle or discipline to do much more than what we felt like doing. Nonetheless, Art, as a reflection of Truth, remained our focus.

Some of us knew we had already "lost." The struggle had consumed us and exhausted our enthusiasm. We limped off the battlefield stunned and confused, but we had shaken the psyche of America. We had captured the attention of mainstream media. They feared us and were determined to see us discredited or marginalized. "Business as usual" was all that mattered. The status quo was being defended and preserved at all costs.

One day, one of our group, Jim Cooney, was poaching eggs and making toast at the farm. He smiled a cunning, coy smile, and said to me, "Even a dead shark can bite off your leg."

But the questions we asked have never been answered: Is this the best we can do? Are we bound to destroy ourselves? Is there a way out?

Some of us thought we had the answers. Or, at least, we thought we had better answers than to keep polluting the planet, carrying on an unjust and unpopular war, and poisoning ourselves with prepackaged foods, only to end up as psychotics hooked on Ritalin or lithium or oxycontin or carbamazepine or ECT (electro-convulsive therapy).

Maybe there are no answers, no way out of our human foibles and flaws. The age of corporate wealth and productivity has created a monster that is devouring us. In the second half of the twentieth century, the monster was unmasked, and we all found ourselves in an era of unprecedented wealth without justice. Spiritually speaking, the monster is an industry of evil fueled by greed, selfishness, a massive confusion of "self-interests," capitalistic enterprise, and opposing intellectual ideologies...*all working in discordance.*

Disease, famine, war, poverty, and injustice, on a worldwide scale, has become "the norm." All our hopes for a clean environment and a just society have been crushed by the real historical thrust of a worldwide consuming economic empire, with more influence than ever before, with a broader, more expansive agenda than ever before.

***

My class of student writers included Dan Carr, who had been writing songs with a band called Cats Cradle. They were high-powered musicians who had cultivated a faithful following. The band was locally known and quite talented. The lead guitar was Michael Gonnick (alias Fly) who later adopted the persona Guru Ganesha Singh. Today, he heads the Guru Ganesha Band. H. Norris was the bass player of Cats Cradle. I have collaborated and worked with him consistently ever since. In 1975, Norris and I produced and recorded in studio the powerful electronic rendition of "Cambodian Spring."

In the same period, I had been contemplating starting a poetry magazine based on what I had learned from Jon Silkin and decided to employ his strategies for distributing and marketing. I had studied the poetry of William Blake and was enamored with his iconoclasm and revolutionary ideas.

The Four Zoas Journal of Poetry and Letters was born. My friend, Bruce, agreed to print the edition, and so the magazine would be both a letterpress project as well as a vehicle to oppose the War in Vietnam and a forum to decry the social injustices of racism, the "war on drugs," and to promote human rights.

Four Zoas Journal 1&2 (Amnesty) was printed at the Morning Star Farm, Jim Cooney's mountaintop sanctuary where he published *The Phoenix*, a literary quarterly. Cooney, an ex-Jesuit and pronounced war resister, was a flamboyant and articulate firebrand for the anti-war movement. I had briefly seen him at a social gathering for Robert Bly at the home of Hui-Ming Wang. But I didn't really meet Cooney until I went with Bruce and Gregory Gillespie to help move a printing press from Cummington Farm to the Morning Star Farm.

***

After my stint at Clark University, I took my stipend and bought a ticket to Jerusalem, with the express purpose of working on an original version of Martin Buber's *I and Thou*. I spent time at Mt. Scopus studying the original text, and I also met with, and interviewed, Ernst Simon, one of Buber's surviving "disciples." I toured Gan Edan, the Golan

Heights, walked the shores of the Kinneret, and traveled into the Negev.

I then flew to Rome and took a train to Perugia, where I lived for several months. I teamed up with a former student from Smith College, and we toured Switzerland together. We traveled to Firenze, generally sharing in our love of art, literature, and each other.

I flew back to the states with a renewed sense of mission but no sense of direction. I knew that I didn't want to teach. I sold my house and formulated a plan to move into the hinterland, live in isolation, and write. I found a rundown farmhouse located on the backside of the Quabbin Reservoir, with 50 acres of woodland and meadows, essentially halfway between Amherst and Worcester Mass. I was enthralled with the mystique of living simply and sanely.

After I'd been Poet in Residence at Clark University, I rented a small storefront (formally a popular vinyl record outlet) right next door to the college. I intended to conduct poetry workshops, sponsor poetry readings, sell books, and provide a space for writers to meet and discuss their work. I maintained the space for several months (though, for the most part, the effort was a failed experiment). I did have one event there that drew a small audience, but otherwise, I had a minimal response or walk-in patronage.

I rented the space from a prominent Italian landlord who was something of a real estate mogul in that section of the city. That first meeting with him to secure the storefront had a special significance. I made an appointment and met him in a haunting factory building, what appeared to have been a "sweat shop" with hundreds of industrial sewing machines lying dormant in eerie silence. He was in his late sixties, a portly man with a somewhat gruff manner—a veritable caricature of a mafia don. His office was an auspicious throne room, and he sat behind a prominently situated desk. I sat in a chair facing him. He appeared skeptical that I wanted to rent the place for poetry readings. He barely comprehended my motive.

I showed him *The Stonecutters* and read a poem from the book. He listened politely as I read, but he still appeared befuddled by what he'd heard or what I was really planning to do in the store. He was still unconvinced. And then, after a moment of thought, told me to come with him.

We left his office and walked back through the graveyard of sewing machines to another door at the far end of the floor. We entered a lavishly decorated "living room," caste in a demure Victorian quietude which had a slight odor of decay as well as preserved elegance—clearly an inner sanctum, an anachronistic mausoleum, as if put together to be a movie set, a depiction of a by-gone era.

Once inside, Mr. P. (with great deference) presented me to an elderly woman, perhaps in her late eighties. He introduced me to his mother. She was sitting on a couch and carried herself with quiet dignity.

Her son explained the present situation, how I wanted to rent the storefront. "He says he's a poet."

She said something to him in Italian. And then

he said, "Okay, go ahead, and read to her like you did before."

I opened the book and read with musical intonation. "When the rock crumbles, there is still a job. Pick up the pieces and reshape the rock. Think of the cracks as…beauty."

She pondered the lines, closed her eyes and repeated them, an echo of what I had read: "Think of the cracks as beauty." With her eyes still closed, she spoke emphatically to her son. "Rent him the store."

***

As the war in Southeast Asia dragged on, news of an ever-expanding illegitimate invasion of Cambodia, coupled with the reality of inhuman destruction, torture, and an ever-growing anti-war resistance at home, provoked me to begin a series of poems under the title *Cambodian Spring*. I believed, and was convinced, that my work had tapped into the very essence of protest while acutely reflecting the quintessential elements of poetic expression.

The poems were immediately published in magazines. Bruce Chandler suggested we make a small edition of the collection as well. Dan Keleher, Bruce Chandler, and myself printed the book at Gehenna Press in the night hours, sleeping on the floor in shifts, passionately committed to our labors.

In 1975, I spent the summer living in a tent with my lover in the woods at the Four Zoas Farm. We were working on a house site, planning to build a geodesic dome. We dug a shallow freshwater well and built a rather large deck. We lived at the site until mid-October. Quixotically, we had acquired a substantial quantity of opium, which we were smoking while blissfully seeking the pleasure of each other. Within myself (and in my exotic opium dreams) I was "retreating into the sanity" of Nature.

I felt determined to escape from the national nightmare of the Vietnam War and the mountain of horrors that the war had promulgated. We went to see a low budget movie, "The Harder They Come," filmed in Jamaica, about a renegade reggae singer. From the opening scene on, I was smitten with the notion of going there. I actually made two trips to the island with every intention of finding a spiritual escape I could believe in. But as much as I loved being there, I also faced the realization that I was inexorably a bona fide U.S. of A. person whose voice and creative power was irrefutably linked to my own nation. My country, right or wrong, was where I ultimately belonged.

Chapter Six

A renowned poet with whom I had been corresponding had high praise for my anti-war poems and invited me to visit him in San Francisco. This is how my relationship with George Oppen began.

In September of 1974, a group of us hand-bound the first *Four Zoas Journal.* George Oppen introduced the magazine with a quintessential statement about the nature of writing effectively and poignantly. I packed up and headed for Atlanta, stopping along the way to sell the *FZ Journal* in the same general way that Jon had done with *STAND.* After several months in Atlanta I took the magazine to D.C., hawking the journal on the streets for three dollars a copy. Most days I sold ten to twenty of them, which generated enough income to keep me in food and a shared apartment with a Corcoran art student. While in D.C. I attended the Watergate trials and began to collect poems and letters for issue number three (entitled "too insane"). William Burroughs suggested the antithetical comment for the front page. (We had struck up a friendship when

I was in New York City on a work trip.) No one had a sharper sense of humor than Burroughs. He was a caustic genius who was both stunningly clever as well as deceptively "sane."

In 1976, the bicentennial year, Jon Silkin and I did a three-month reading tour together. We traveled to New York City, out to Ithaca, New York, then on to readings in Connecticut, New Hampshire, and Massachusetts.

That summer, during the New York Book Fair, I met Gerard Malanga. We struck up an immediate friendship and rapport that was both professional and forged in profound synchronicity. We were contemporaries. We shared a deep connection to the art we practiced as well as the way we forged our careers to reflect our definite poetic values and creative dispositions.

Gerard, once affiliated with Andy Warhol, had established himself as a respected photo archivist and a formidably published poet. He was especially supportive of my writing and put his own prestige on the line to promote my poetry. He also visited the Four Zoas Farm and became the official photographer and chronicler of what we were doing there. Beyond that, he made overtures to a number of presses to see my work published in a major format. He even went so far as to type a manuscript of 128 pages of my work, which he submitted to several prominent publishing houses. Ultimately, he landed a book deal for me with Kulchur Press. *Let Myself Shine* was published in 1979.

In 1970, I got hold of Gregor-Smith's translation of Martin Buber's *Ich und Du*, a challenging if not convoluted examination of Man's relationship to God (I and Thou).

Reading the text, I was both mystified and smitten but could not comprehend the substance of what Buber was actually intimating. Buber thought Gregor-Smith's version was accurate but too rigid. After years of study and thought given to the dynamic ideas posited in his construct of "Relation," another version of Buber's text was issued in a new translation by Walter Kaufman (after Buber's death). One clear change offered a key ingredient to the overall problem. I and Thou is a blatant mistranslation. *Du* in German is the familiar second person (singular). Kaufman's translation of the title more accurately reflects the spiritual intent: *I and You*.

I felt spurred on by my unquenched desire to experience the reality of the I-YOU Relation, whatever that involved or required. I began an exhaustive "transliteration" of the original text and used the two available translations for comparison. I became dedicated to the task of seeing beyond the literal value of the book and delved more and more into the phenomenon of the I-YOU awareness. The process became a priori poetic inversion. So, instead of counting from one to Infinity (which can never be accomplished) the task was to start with Infinity and arrive at the I-YOU Relationship. While in Israel, in 1972, I spent an afternoon with Ernst Simon. He was very helpful, and I gleaned what I could from his recollections of Martin Buber, the man, the teacher, the prophetic voice of a vibrant existential spirituality. Simon specifically referred to himself as a 'disciple' of his mentor and colleague. He spoke at length regarding the Doctrine of Absorption, and the confusion created by our language and conceptual thinking. Buber had established that *Being* as an abstraction of the mind is another "It." I-You is pure Being.

The first draft of my original version of the I-YOU manuscript, my poemic transliteration, took the better part of a year to complete. But I was still unable to grasp that the I-YOU Dialogic existed outside the boundaries of intellectual pursuit, which means, I was trapped in the IT-Mind thinking about YOU.

My line-by-line transliteration of *I and YOU* was finished in 1980. My first draft had taken the better part of a year to complete, but my manuscript seemed lifeless, clinical, and no closer to revealing any real "new" or explosive insight into what Buber had put forth. Only my stubborn insistence had brought me as far as I had gotten. I was ready to abandon the endeavor altogether. I shelved the project and moved on with only the remotest notion that I might one day return to the manuscript.

Then, twelve years later, in 1992, while reviewing the text and meditating on why the work I had done never resulted in either an original approach to the text or a revelation of Buber's essential truth, I had a singular moment when I was able to reconfigure the conceptual core of the dialogic, the reality of the "two fold nature" of I and You.

I saw in a metaphoric visualization an intuitive moment of clarity as I stood at the south slope of

Tynmouth Mountain gazing into the deeply wooded landscape. Existential Being is YOU. I and You *is* Being. IT exists but has no being. I was spiritually transformed from an I-IT relational state to an I-YOU awareness.

I rushed back to my studio like Archimedes running through the streets naked yelling, "Eureka!" The raw manuscript was the block of marble I would strip to its core to reveal its essence, or more accurately, its obscured and latently dynamic spiritual meaning.

I transformed the manuscript into a living or "present" utterance of Being, not held back or mutated by IT. My own writing would also come to give voice to a new freedom, an awakened voice, a voice reflecting the essential natures of language and meaning as revealed in the human need to conceptualize Being and see beyond the "World of IT."

In 1977, I returned from San Francisco after my second visit with George Oppen. I was offered a poetry reading at a small venue in Worcester, Mass. at the *Garden of Delights*, an alternative vegetarian restaurant and hangout for all kinds of artists and "hippies." My reading was low key if not unprofitable. I made eight dollars passing the hat and sold one journal. I was disgusted and kicking myself for having taken the gig. I packed up and was planning a quick exit when a pair of long legs and a soft voice stood between me and the door.

"I really liked your poems." I was in no mood for any social discourse.

I tersely replied as I looked into her eyes. "I suppose you'd like a ride home?"

"That would be nice," she said.

I was both disarmed and smitten.

I was thirty-two and she was twenty-five. Her name, Rosemary Dredge—a struggling artist who worked at the restaurant as a cook and waitress.

My relationship with Rosemary was founded on our mutual artistic interests. She was also a gifted musician. She was beautiful, naturally athletic, adventurous, and plucky.

She'd worked for a time at Second City in Chicago. Our relationship was driven by the challenge to create books together. She believed in the mission of The Four Zoas Press.

Our bond was not founded on romantic notions nor were we "in love." In those days, she was an avowed atheist. I was an agnostic. So, at least in that area, we generally agreed that religion was neither part of our conversation nor of any importance in the Art we produced. She'd enrolled in Worcester Art College and worked as a baker and waitress (part-time), earning just enough to pay her rent and buy food. She did not have a car.

For the better part of a year I had been commuting from Hardwick to Worcester to work with Harry Norris on musical collaborations, the most notable being the electronic orchestration of *Cambodian Spring* (as well as other songs we had written together), so I'd see Rosemary on those trips. At other times she got rides out to Hardwick. After a year or so of letter-writing and working at the press, we began a serious courtship.

We married in January 1978 in a civil ceremony in Springfield, Mass. We moved into the Four Zoas farmhouse and set up a letterpress printing shop and studio. We established a new imprint, Jerusalem House, for our own projects, printing only very limited editions on hand-made rag papers using a Ben Franklin treadle press.

Other projects included publishing a wide range of contemporary poets, produced at our shop in Ware, Mass. (poetry by Morgan Gibson, Don Quatrale, Ilka Skobie, Barry Lee, among others). Those projects were printed and published under The Four Zoas Press imprint (including two books of poems by Andrei Codescru (printed by Dan Carr in Charlestown). For our honeymoon Rosemary and I traveled across the country on tour, reading poetry, singing songs at a variety of venues, and selling the books we had printed.

We sold our work in NYC and D.C. and then headed west, traveling across the country in a pick-up truck laden with our musical instruments, sleeping bags, and boxes of Four Zoas books. We performed songs together, crossed the Rockies, saw the Grand Canyon, and traversed Death Valley.

We landed in L.A. where her father, Bill Dredge, lived in a small three-room apartment in Redondo Beach. Bill graciously gave us his bedroom and he slept on the couch. Bill didn't own a television. For entertainment we played music on his turntable. His collection of Jazz was extensive, including all the vinyl recordings of Charlie Parker. When not in the apartment, Rose and I spent our days visiting art galleries, going to the movies, walking on the beach, and eating Mexican food. And we sold books in Hollywood to a prominent bookstore in the vicinity. We spent two weeks with her dad, culminating in a wild ride with him in his VW bus to the Baja. Along the way we spent an afternoon at the Monastery at Capistrano.

Bill Dredge had served as an officer aboard a submarine in the south Pacific during World War II. Subs had to resurface every two or three days to replenish their oxygen. They had standing orders to sink any boats and kill all witnesses who saw them. Many of those "witnesses" were unarmed fishing vessels, sometimes populated by peasants who lived on their boats with their families (including their parents and their children). They were all gunned down, slaughtered mercilessly. The strategy assumed that even those who were not enemies might tell the Japanese they'd seen an American sub.

Bill came home from the war eaten up inside by what he'd been complicit in perpetrating, in his mind, the wholesale slaughter of innocent by-standers. He hated what he'd done, and he resented the government that ordered him to do it.

So, he'd bought land in the Baja and intended to build a house there. He was determined to become an ex-patriot, to protest the defilement to his soul and cope with the guilt he lived with every day. He looked me squarely in the eyes and told me he could hardly stand to live with himself. Every day, he saw the faces of those he murdered staring back at him. To make matters worse, he was awarded medals for bravery and heroism beyond the call of duty. The government (and the military) had swept the reality of the war in the Pacific into an untold, unacknowledged secret, never to be spoken of, never to be resolved.

Bill's best friend, Leonard Wibberly, was a well-published Irish novelist who'd been an outspoken radical ever since his days as a partisan fighting against the Fascist dictatorship of Franco in Spain. After the "Freedom of Information Act" was passed, Leonard went to Washington and asked to see any files the U.S. government had against him. He was shocked when he was shown three dollies full of surveillance memos, phone taps, reports, and investigative reports.

He came over on a Friday for an evening and the four of us were fully engaged, discussing geo-politics, fascism, "the war," the Kennedy assassination—in other words, the full range of controversial subjects that fueled our creative interests. Toward evening, Leonard's wife dropped in and invited us to an ice cream social.

Bill and Leonard would have none of it. They'd already planned a night out on the town. Rose and I were headed off to the movies. So Leonard's wife, after some discussion about getting Leonard home at a descent hour, graciously bowed out and they all left around seven p.m.

Sometime around two in the morning, Leonard and Bill returned to the apartment. They'd obviously been revving up and were still going at it. The bar was open. That evening is virtually recreated in the only stage play I wrote, *The Night the Mouse Roared*, a scathing and cathartic dose of the demons and phantoms that possessed those two authors. I wrote the final script in 1998, twenty years after the episodic events of 1978, and I withheld the script until 2008. I did so because there was enough to their life experiences to make me respectful of the controversial and intimate nature of what I had revealed. Leonard was the renowned author of *The Mouse That Roared*. He and Bill had conceived the plot on a drunken binge in Tijuana.

Tully Bascomb—played by Peter Sellers in the movie version—leads an army of medieval knights armed with crossbows to declare war on and invade the United States. They're hoping to lose and thus be eligible for foreign aide. They actually win the war, capturing the "Cobalt Bomb." The nations of the world are forced to disarm their nuclear weapons.

During the summer of 1979, with our infant son still in diapers, Rose and I worked at the shop in Charlestown (we had sublet an apartment in Lynn). Every other week we commuted back to the farm to rest as well as enjoy the creative invigoration of our sanctuary.

In 1980, we signed over The Four Zoas to Dan and focused exclusively on Jerusalem House. We published two major projects, *Big Meadow / New River* and *According to Josephus*, both printed by hand in Hardwick at the farmhouse. My poems and R. M. Dredge's hand-cut woodblocks were serendipitous expressions of our collaborative partnership.

Our second child was born at home in June 1980. That same year we sold the farmhouse, and I took a job as Headmaster of a small private home school program. Two months into the job the funding for the program was gutted when the voters passed Proposition Two. I was "let go."

We had some savings left from selling the farm, so we bought a van and decided to head west in search of a new home. After a month of camping and touring, we made our way to La Mision in Baja, California where Bill had built his dream house. We stayed only long enough to recover from the long ride and the disappointment of our failed hegira. Rosemary was now carrying our third child. On the return trip we crossed the Gila Flats, traveling east. We stopped in Asheville, N.C., where, to my amazement, I was received with accolades and fanfare. We made about $2,000 selling our books in a matter of days. We immediately rented an old farmhouse nearby, between Mars Hill and Marshall. We hunkered down near the French Broad not far from Campobello. It was springtime in the Smokey Mountains.

Chapter Seven

After making another windfall of cash in real estate (in 1984) we made yet another attempt to relocate, this time moving back to California to a remote town in the Sierras on the chaparral, in Ramona, where we rented a house. It was close enough to the Baja to make frequent trips to La Mision to visit Bill. On Bill's refrigerator was a cartoon cutout from the New Yorker Magazine depicting two men with satellite dishes next to their houses. One turns to the other and says, "Would you believe, there's nothing on in the whole world."

We kept ponies, grew a garden, and spent most of our time enjoying our children and being in love with each other. I turned forty that spring. I was happy, fit, mentally acute and more in love with Rosemary than ever. Rosemary was thirty-two. In Ramona, we conceived our fifth child.

We still had one four-acre parcel of land in Hardwick. We returned to Massachusetts with a plan to build a house and settle down to raise our children, but the economics of the moment were not favorable to start a construction project. I hadn't made any money in almost a year. So, when I was offered a long-term substitute position as Department Chair teaching two courses of Literature at a local high school, the timing seemed providential. That short-term appointment turned into a three-year teaching stint.

We sold the property and set our sights on buying land in Vermont. During that time of transition I began to work on a novel, and continued with slow and steady progress on what became a longer project, *The Saga of King Philip*. I had set my mind to writing a novel years earlier, but I did not have the staying power, the time, or the know-how to sustain hundreds of pages of prose. I was a poet with a family to care for and no sense of a tangible permanence or what the future would look like. But our vision was still a vibrant one, to escape from a life of complacency and embrace with all our passion, a meaningful way forward.

After doing research and reading through the real estate classified ads in Vermont, we packed up our five children and drove up Rt. 103 to Rt. 141, passing White Rocks and then over Tynmouth Mountain into Middletown Springs, a town without a traffic light and a population of about three hundred. We came to an eleven-acre parcel of meadow and forest on a mountain slope facing south right on the Poultney River. Our children frolicked in the woods, we picnicked and napped in the sunny April afternoon, and we bought the land that same day.

We established a summer camp. We would continue to live in the city, raise our children while I taught poetry at the high school (finishing the contract for that school year). That was the year the shuttle exploded while all of us watched it happen on TV.

That summer we made frequent trips up to our place in Vermont. Summer in Vermont was idyllic. We went swimming in the Poultney River and on the Fourth of July, in Poultney, we watched the fireworks with our family huddled on a blanket in the grass.

Our homesite was well-established. We had a camper that slept four comfortably. I had built an outhouse and a little two-room tool shed which we also used as a rough kitchen and bunkhouse. We picked blackberries. We hiked the deer trails, explored the caves, and carried buckets of water from a freshwater pond so we could wash the dishes.

In 1985, I was offered an adjunct teaching position at Castleton State College, twenty-five miles north of our place in the Green Mountains. It was a low-paying slot, but it seemed to be our plausible opportunity to escape the city altogether and build a house on our land. All seemed within our grasp.

I went on three selling tours, two trips to New York City and one to Washington D.C. I sold my books of poetry to libraries and private collectors, book dealers and bookstores.

The money from those selling tours was set aside to buy the building materials for the house we envisioned…a small, six room energy-efficient "arc" plunked on the ledge of the mountain inside the tree line, a quarter of a mile up from the paved road.

That first summer, our whole family vacationed at the camp, and we all worked to clear the site for the house.

The first year of construction I worked alone. I taught one course at the college Tuesday and Thursday afternoon. I would drive up from Massachusetts for a three-day stretch.

I worked the site, prepared the foundation, and moved materials into the woods by hand. On Thursdays, I drove back to Massachusetts. That next spring, we rented a house in near-by Poultney, one town south of the college and just north of our house-site. We packed up everything we owned and moved to Vermont.

Later that same summer, we moved into our place. The kitchen was functional but most of the rooms were still under construction. I hired on a small crew of carpenters, as well as a plumber and an electrician, to hurry along the work.

We were eating food grown in our own garden. I kept chickens. We heated with wood. Rosemary baked a variety of breads, muffins, and pies. We swam in the river. We landscaped the terrain. Those were our "good old days."

We saw a chance to raise our children in rural peace. We belonged to a home school network. We were living on the cusp of a virtual wilderness. Deer and bear roamed our property.

In one of our rooms, we planned to have a studio space. I had stored boxes of printed materials, letters, and manuscripts from the Four

Zoas Press. Rosemary wanted to convert the room into a bedroom for our oldest son. She gave me an ultimatum. Get rid of the boxes.

What should I do with them? She told me for all she cared, I could put them in our car and drive them down to the river. She wasn't making a joke or willing to change her mind. I drove down to town and called Gil Williams (in Binghamton, N.Y.), a long-standing buyer and supporter of my work. I explained to him my predicament. He proposed an immediate solution. He would buy one or two boxes, sight unseen, and donate them to SUNY Buffalo, establishing an archive there. Robert Bertholt, the special collections librarian, agreed to take the entire lot. When I came back home and told Rosemary I'd sold all the boxes, she was stunned and speechless. The look on her face was worth far more than the significant boon we got for the archives.

We were tucked in and where we wanted to be. I was teaching several courses at the college. We had built our dream into a reality. But there were negative consequences we hadn't foreseen. First, the economy had become very inflated. Money just didn't spend like it once had. We needed a second income. Rosemary had to go back to work as an elementary school substitute teacher. We gave up on home school and sent the children to public school. Second, and even more absolute, we experienced culture shock. We were far from family and in a remote setting, dislocated from our roots in urban/suburban living.

I was teaching more classes, so I maintained more of a cultural connection through campus life, but Rosemary had become locked into a life at home. We were miles from town. We had no neighbors in sight of our home. She felt worn down, isolated and trapped.

I converted the camper in the back yard into my writing studio. I was still having my poems published in many magazines, including the *Vermont Literary Review* and *STAND Magazine*. I also received a sizeable stipend for writing the shooting script for a French feature film. I was also commissioned to publish and print a limited edition facsimile copy of one of Basquait's notebooks (after his death) for a major show in New York City. That project was arranged through Gerard Malanga.

***

1990. Several major life-bending events and a sequence of setbacks fell upon us. Rosemary's dad became gravely ill with cancer. She flew out to be with him at his home in La Mision. She took our youngest daughter, then two years old, with her. I stayed in Vermont with our older four. Bill died a few months later at seventy-six years old. We were devastated with grief.

December 1990. I contracted a severe eye infection, which attacked my retinas, blinding me. The doctor diagnosed me and administered drops, bandaging my eyes and sending me home. He told me he'd remove the bandages in two weeks. At that time he would know whether or not the damage was permanent or whether the macro-regeneration process would restore my sight.

I was confronted with fear and uncertainty. I spent two days in bed, like a helpless invalid. On the third day I rediscovered a courage within me to face the fact that I might never see again. I realized I knew the house implicitly, and could count the steps to the kitchen and bathroom. I figured out how to boil water and make tea. Within a few days, my hearing had become acute, so much so that I could tell who was walking near me simply by the sound of their feet. When the doctor removed the bandages, I could "see" but my eyes were no longer as they had been. I needed glasses and I could not see much at all at night. Mortal certainty had caught up with me.

That summer Rosemary and I were confronted with an unplanned pregnancy. We were going to have a sixth child.

In an early visit for a prenatal exam, her doctor gave us a stark diagnosis. He found that Rose had a serious blood-clotting condition (phlebitis) and urged us to consider aborting the pregnancy. We went home dismayed and facing a horrendous dilemma. We spent two days mulling over what we were confronting. Either risk Rosemary's life in carrying the baby to term or have an abortion, which the doctor was advocating. We were faced with the choice neither of us wanted to make. Her life was in the balance.

I certainly did not want to consider the real possibility that I might have to raise five children without their mother.

I would have supported Rosemary's decision if she had wanted to terminate her pregnancy. We chose to have the baby. I took on all the household tasks, doing the laundry, cleaning the house, cooking the meals, shopping for the groceries, and getting the children to their after-school activities.

Rose would rest, stay in bed as much as possible, adhere to a diet of healthy foods, and all the while, keep herself mentally positive.

Nine months later, my mother suffered a brain hemorrhage in her sleep and never woke up. We buried her on May 6th.

Our sixth baby was born two weeks later. We rejoiced to see our child, a fourth daughter, born healthy, while grieving my mother's death at the same time. Our sense of composure had been shredded. Rose's father and my mother were the emotional glue that connected us to family and a sense of security. I was forty-five. Rosemary was thirty-eight. We were no longer young, carefree, or certain about where we were and why we were there.

One evening, after we'd put the children to sleep and Rose had gone to read in our bedroom, I stealthily prepared a gourmet meal for us. I set out our best plates, lit a candle, and invited her down for a late night supper. Since we lived far off in the boonies and really didn't have the income to go out so much as we would have liked, this was my way of creating a time just for the two of us to discuss intimately whatever was on our minds.

She seemed pleasantly surprised, and genuinely impressed with the fuss I exhibited to show her I really cared. After twelve years together, I was still madly in love, happy to have a home, thankful for our children, and hunkering down for the long haul through middle age. I was still fit and sassy. Rose looked vibrant and lovely.

We sipped our wine and ate our meal. Our conversation focused on what we should do to improve our lives, what direction we ought to consider, what we should do to make progress. We wanted to plan for the future.

Rosemary had become less and less enchanted with where we'd settled. We talked about selling the house and land. But I was skeptical about finding work elsewhere, or giving up all we'd worked for. What we'd accomplished had been notable.

Then Rosemary stated with absolute certainty that it all meant nothing.

"Then what's it all about?" I asked.

"What about being *saved*?"

My thoughts had been consumed with how to get the kids grown up and off to college, and how to keep us healthy so we could have some measure of our youthful desires as we reached our middle years, and that we'd have something left to enjoy our old age together.

But "being saved" was not in my lexicon. I stared into her soul and knew she was being absolutely serious.

"What do you mean? How do we work that out?"

"What about being forgiven for our sins? What are you going to say to answer for yourself after you die, when you face judgment? And what about our children? What about their eternal souls?" Rosemary asked.

"Do you mean, after we're dead?"

"I'm talking about after this life. When we are called to account for our actions and our choices."

"Rosemary, I don't believe in life after death. I just want to be a responsible adult. Live a decent life. Love you. Take care of our children. That's enough. Isn't it?"

"No, it's not. It's not about now, or living a good life. It's about what happens to our eternal souls."

Rosemary was in distress—a spiritual crisis. She wanted to rediscover her connection to a religious meaning. Some of her friends in town invited her to attend a Protestant church with them. I was content to stay on a secular path. I didn't need or want a religious life. I certainly had no interest in attending church. But I made no objection to her wanting to do so. And I conceded to her desire to expose the children to what the church offered. She dressed them up and they went to Sunday services. I weighed what the effect might be on our children, and I concluded that they would make their own decisions to accept or reject what they experienced, if not right away, certainly when they were old enough to think for themselves. I spent my Sundays working on various projects around the house. I built an expansive deck. I enjoyed having the undistracted time to myself.

What came next caused me to regret remaining aloof from Rosemary's deep longings to find her answers in a religious doctrine. Her faith had become fanatical. She gave me an ultimatum. Either I convert to Christianity and attend church with the family or she would leave me. I was dumfounded and stunned by her adamant and absolute line in the sand.

I was a non-practicing Jew. I hated religious ritual and had no belief in the literal, historical Bible. I certainly did not believe in a resurrected man or a god who impregnated himself into a woman. We'd had our share of disagreements, disappointments, and disillusionments, but we'd always been able to find a way to reconcile our love for our children and each other.

We had remained faithful and supportive of one another. This was an impasse neither of us could overcome. I could not, and would not, comply with her demand. After fourteen years of marriage, we were on the verge of divorce.

Chapter Eight

We'd reached a point of stark, irreconcilable difference. Rosemary packed her bags and moved out, taking four of our six children with her. Two of the children stayed with me, by their own choice.

Our relationship was damaged beyond repair. We became bitter with each other. Two years later, having lived apart with no civility left between us, we divorced by mutual consent.

If only for the sake of our children, our divorce agreement was mutually constructed without lawyers. We agreed that we would share joint, legal custody and exchanges of children for visits and vacations. She ceded the house and property to me, and I agreed to support her financial needs, as much as was reasonable and practical.

Two years after our break-up we were hardly speaking to one another. She had left the church and had fallen into despair. She was exhausted by the ordeal of raising four children. We spoke about me assuming physical custody of all the children.

On the door to her apartment hung a sign that read, "Jesus loves you." My heart was broken. I could not comprehend what nourishment she derived from what she professed to believe. Jesus wasn't working for her. She was alone, suffering, and still adamantly committed to being saved.

Rosemary had become harried and desperate. The pressures of single-parenting, a boss who was putting unreasonable demands on her to work weekends, and mismanaging what money she did have, all contributed to a dire situation. She called me and told me she was contemplating suicide. I intervened as best I could, assuring her I would take all the children to live with me while she went into a decent treatment facility.

Whether as a coincidence or simply because Rosemary was desperately hanging on to her faith, she accepted an invitation to have dinner at The Twelve Tribes household, located diagonally across the street from her apartment. Also known as the Church of Island Pond or the Messianic Communities, they were a communal society of fundamentalist believers who maintained a 24/7 lifestyle that was both provocative and controversial.

The members wooed her and suggested she sell her possessions and move in with them. They invited her to attend a wedding in Boston at another household populated by members. She took the four girls with her, therefore failing to honor my scheduled visit for that weekend with two of my daughters. And she never informed me or asked me for my okay.

I showed up on schedule to pick up my two daughters for their regularly scheduled sleepover. I was angry that she had taken them to Boston, but beyond that, my internal alarm bells were activated.

When she returned from Boston, she called me, flatly stating that she had joined the Twelve Tribes and the children would no longer be coming for visits as the "community" did not allow their children to go "out into the world." Not only was Rosemary breaking her legally binding custody agreement, but she wasn't speaking for herself anymore, nor acting on her own decisions.

That very Sunday, I was having coffee at a local favorite restaurant, frequented by most of the college professors and lawyers. I saw a friend across the way who happened to be a somewhat renowned journalist, and I asked her about the Twelve Tribes. She told me they were "a dangerous cult" who were known to abuse children by caning them for disobediences. She also warned me that they were capable of spiriting children out of the country to other Twelve Tribe communities in Brazil or Argentina. She knew of one father who had not seen his daughter in more than ten years and had given up searching for her.

A local police officer called me (off the record) after hearing that my ex-wife had joined the "cult." He told me that the police were hoping to do to the Twelve Tribes what had been done to the Davidians in Waco.

I was horrified by his comment. I had always been a First Amendment advocate. I believe in freedom of religion (or the freedom to not believe in any religion). But my children were in that house, and a policeman had just told me they'd like to burn down the house my children were living in. I was determined to get them out of there. I sped down the mountain, and with no desire to "work it out" with Rose. The thought that my children might be whipped or beaten by cult members made me livid.

I pulled up in front of the Twelve Tribes house. Some of their members seemed pleasant, even hospitable, and I casually walked up on to the porch. Rosemary and the girls came out to greet me. They all looked healthy enough, but Rosemary was still refusing to "allow" the children to come for their scheduled visits. I was invited to come into the house for a discussion, but before I got to the door one of my daughters, then seven years old, pulled me aside and quietly whispered in my ear, "Daddy, I don't want to be here. A man choked me and locked me in a closet."

That was enough. I didn't need to have a more involved conversation. I ordered the girls to get in the car. Whatever else I might tolerate, I would not leave my daughters to be "disciplined" or "trained" by these religious fanatics. I took the children and refused to return them. Rosemary filed charges against me for violating the custody agreement. I removed the children from Rutland County and hired an attorney to argue before a judge to rule in my favor, that to return the girls was to put them in danger and cause them psychological harm.

The courtroom drama made national news, but the case was especially impacting in the Rutland-Burlington press.

In 1984, the infamous "raid" on the Island Pond Church by Vermont state authorities was still fomenting. The police had arrested many of the church members and had removed the children in a sweeping round-up, alleging "child abuse" by the church. Within days the case was nullified, as a judge ruled that "the church" could not be held responsible for individual acts of abuse by parents. As each parent was brought before the court, there was not one witness nor any physical evidence to support the charges. All the charges against the parents were dismissed. The children were returned to their parents.

Although The Twelve Tribes had "escaped the law" on a technicality, the police, the news media, and the political office holders believed the Twelve Tribes was guilty of child abuse.

The sensationalism of our custody trial, combined with the wrenching emotional ordeal of the courtroom "battle," resulted in exhaustion and trauma for all of us. I won in court. I was awarded legal and physical custody of all our children. In the final settlement, the Twelve Tribes lawyer wanted a signed document that specifically stipulated that children in the community were raised "differently" but were not abused.

I took my six children home and spent the next year single-parenting, teaching full-time, keeping house, and cooking meals. I wanted life to be good for my children, but the girls missed being with their mother. There was no way to ignore the emotional turmoil we were all experiencing. One by one the girls wanted to go back to the community. They just wanted to be with their mother. The oldest three of my daughters went to live with Rosemary, one after the other in the coming year. I still held legal custody so I was able to maintain an open door into their lives. I insisted on one explicit condition: no one was to discipline my children except Rosemary.

***

In 1996, Rosemary was diagnosed with advanced breast cancer. A year or two earlier, she'd had a lumpectomy and the doctor determined that the lump was benign. Her prognosis was dire. The doctor told her she would live four months to one year with or without treatments. He suggested radical surgery, radiation, and chemotherapy.

Rose battled her cancer without the aggressive actions suggested by the doctor. She started fasting, eating only live foods and fresh made vegetable juices. She was undaunted in her faith. In the first year, the tumor in her breast shrunk from the size of a fist to a thumbnail. In 1999, her body was no longer able to fight off the advancing disease. Tumors had spread throughout her body.

I had spent a semester away from teaching. I bought a small residential space in Florida so that I was free to spend my time writing poetry, tucked into my studio in Hallandale, Florida. The poem *OUTERMOST A Man Alone* (later published in China) typified my work at the time—objectivist, lean, macroscopic, evoking the eternal pulse of the I-YOU dialogic. My writing was transformative, wrapped in a language of isolation that was fresh, awake, and immediately accessible. I was also being drawn more than ever toward Nature as the primary source of inspired creativity.

Both my sons had gone off to college. All four of my daughters were living with their mother on the Twelve Tribes farm in Cambridge, New York. I received a call from Rosemary in June. She was very sick. She'd taken a turn for the worst. She wanted to see me immediately. I booked myself on to the auto-train and arrived in New York within twenty-four hours of our conversation.

The sun felt warm on my face. There was a sweet breeze coming out of the west. Rosemary and I sat on a hillside looking into each other's eyes. She looked as beautiful as ever, but the telling signs of how the cancer had damaged her were evident. She reiterated her condition...a matter of weeks, possibly months.

The point being—and what weighed on her utterly—what was to happen to the girls?

I listened to everything she said, internalizing what we were confronting, but I hadn't reacted or stated what I was thinking. I already knew the answer, but I held back. I tempered my answer to be as gentle as I could, in how I spoke and what I was intending. I told her the older girls could do what they wanted. The two younger girls would be living with me. The unspoken truth: I had no intention of letting my older daughters stay in the community once their mother was...deceased. The situation seemed steeped in surreality, a discussion about her probable death, the time when her life would be over.

I drove north and set up a campsite at Lake St. Catherine. I was on the schedule to teach several courses at Castleton starting in August. I felt glad to be going back, as my funds were depleted, having used most of my savings in the previous six months. I had been "off the clock," working as a full-time writer.

I liked to drive the back roads between Cambridge and Middletown Springs, through the Green Mountains. The veldt-like expanses along the Mattawan River and lush country of rolling meadows were framed against the backdrop of rugged mountains, back trails, hidden waterfalls, and deep woodlands where wilderness and farmland blended into a panorama, an aesthetic of meta-psychic energy. There was refreshment and peace at a time of horrendous imposing tragedy.

One dramatic ride cut west from Dorset over a high trail and dropped down into Salem, New York, just one town north of Cambridge. All through those months I had been writing poems culled from those excursions, poems infused with Nature and deep probing thoughts about the palpable meaning of life.

I was fifty-four years old and considering very seriously that I would buy acreage on the backside of "Dead Man's Alley" between Rupert and Dorset, where I intended to build a house, in the remote, rural serenity of "God's country."

Rosemary's condition weighed heavily in my thoughts. But the focus of my concerns was fixed primarily on my daughters' well-being. I felt determined to re-assert myself back into their lives on a daily basis, while making every effort to be considerate of Rosemary's fragile and precarious condition. She was gravely ill and growing weaker.

I was spending all of my free time in Cambridge, eating meals with the girls, pitching in with farm chores (repairing fences, shucking corn, stacking firewood) and monitoring the care Rosemary was receiving. On a few occasions I had engaged the group "leaders" to consider seeking sound advice from a doctor with more expertise. A cancer specialist came from Albany to examine her. He prescribed liquid roxinal and opium patches to ease her pain.

Somehow, through that time of Rosemary's impending death, we still held a spark of love for each other, but given the situation, we agreed to focus all our attention on the children. I had all but "moved in" to the community.

In November, Rosemary's condition was critical. Her death seemed imminent, perhaps only days away. She was very weak, unable to keep any food down, and her pain was excruciating. The entire community was poised to accept her passing. Inexplicably, at that last hour, she had a dramatic remission. Within twenty-four hours she was alert, hungry, smiling, and wanted to get outside for some fresh air.

Although the onslaught of Rosemary's cancer was in remission, she was still very weak, her body ravaged by tumors, and she was still suffering with inordinate pain.

She had become more reclusive, somewhat anti-social, and resigned to her suffering.

In mid-November she had taken a solitary walk up a dirt road toward the cow barn. She slipped in the thawing mud, wrenching her thigh and hip. She was unable to get up or walk back to her room. Humiliated and alone, she waited to be rescued. She was carried back to her house. After that she did not leave her bed for any reason.

I visited her in her room and had a caustic exchange about the well-being of the girls. We were both arguing and bringing up old resentments. We agreed that we would not speak to each other for a time. Any necessary communication between us was to be done through her spiritual leader, who was trying to be objective and fair to both of us.

About two weeks passed without any positive communication between us, when I was told that Rosemary wanted to see me. I went to visit her in her room. She was clearly shaken (or subdued) and seemed to be genuinely contrite about the spat we'd had. She specifically apologized for walking out on our marriage. What I could not determine was whether her sincerity stemmed from the drugs she was taking which made her more submissive, or did she, in fact, have a genuine desire to "repent" because death was pressing in upon her. I was bowled over, completely disarmed and stupefied. I really didn't know what to say.

My heart was turned toward her, as once we had been devoted parents and partners, lovers and best friends. It was as if after eight years of haranguing and bickering and spitting fire at each other we saw a way to be cleansed and purified in the sweetness of her swan song and my desire to honor her in her last days by caring for her and holding back nothing.

***

We remarried in February 2000. I went to the town hall and filed a marriage license. Paid the fee. Three days later, after a small family gathering and celebration, we moved into a bedroom in the farmhouse at the edge of White Creek where we spent the next eight months together.

Rosemary died in my arms on Sunday, October 8th, 2000, at four in the morning. She was forty-eight years old. We had spent the last days and hours together in our bedroom in the farmhouse. Our doctor arrived shortly thereafter and examined her body, determining her death had been caused by heart failure due to a massive tumor pressing against her heart.

Later that morning, she was swaddled in her blankets and her body placed in a simple wooden coffin which was transported to Island Pond, Vermont, where her remains were interred at a small ceremony attended by a few friends and my son Matthew, who'd traveled from his college. He wept on my shoulder. The two of us covered the earth over her.

Her death was a devastating blow to all of my children. It was left to me to guard over the well-being of my four daughters. They were emotionally devastated. I hardly had an opportunity to mourn. All my strength was focused on the children.

I was reeling with grief and slipping into a

nihilistic malaise. I made a conscious decision to remain in the Twelve Tribes as a way to maintain a sane and stable environment for my daughters. The situation was complicated by our need to grieve and regroup as a family.

My love for Rosemary had never been more complete as in those last months and weeks as we faced what we knew would be her passing. The inevitable and the inexorable fused, and what resulted was a deeper bond between us. I wanted her death to mean something beyond the grief we were all bearing, and all of us needed to keep a cohesive grip on living in a way that preserved her memory, and gave credible substance to her life, that she hadn't died in vain. Ultimately, it took me ten years to move beyond her passing.

Chapter Nine

My opposition to the death penalty formed in college, and over the decades, I remained steadfast in my conviction, premised on one important truth—that innocent people are executed because of false evidence, mistaken eye-witness testimony, and misrepresentation of mitigating circumstances. Poor people and people of color are more frequently executed.

On August 23rd, 1927, Fernandino Sacco and Bartholomeo Vanzetti were executed in Massachusetts after being found guilty of a murder/robbery of a factory payroll in Braintree. They were Italian immigrant targeted as communist agitators, union members, and anarchists. They were innocent, and the case against them was entirely fabricated with perjured testimony, false evidence planted by the police, and sensational, inflammatory newspaper reporting.

When Ethel and Julius Rosenberg were charged with espionage, I was only seven years old. The Russians exploded a nuclear bomb. The case against the Rosenbergs was that they'd given "the secret" of the bomb to the Russians (even though it was widely known that the Soviets had imported a slew of Nazi scientists, just as the U.S. had done at the end of World War II).

Julius was a TV repairman who worked with electronics. Both he and his wife Ethel had been active in the American communist party, and they were Jews. But they had no access to secrets about atomic bomb production. In fact, there was no secret to pass on. Building an atom bomb required an industry of laboratory steps, all of which were known among most nuclear scientists.

The government's case was almost totally based on the testimony of Julius's brother-in-law, Morton Sobell, who had worked as a low level engineer at a manufacturing facility producing minor components for centrifuges. He was given a lesser sentence in return for his damning testimony against Ethel and Julius. Found guilty, they were sentenced to death and executed by electrocution. Ethel had to be executed twice because the first shock did not stop her heart. A phone had been placed by the death chamber connected to President Eisenhower. If they would confess, their sentence would be commuted. Ethel would not agree to the deal and chose to die rather than admit to any guilt. Their two sons were secretly taken in by a Jewish family living in Springfield, Massachusetts. Their last names were changed.

In 1990, I wrote a series of articles about a Vermont man who languished on death row in Texas for more than ten years and was about to be put to death even though there was ample evidence to show he hadn't committed the murder. He'd been convicted, in part, because police suppressed evidence showing his probable innocence.

In court, an eyewitness testified that she'd seen Bobby Drew slash her boyfriend's throat. But soon after the trial, she admitted that she hadn't seen the murder. The police pressured her into testifying against Drew to make sure there would be an insurmountable case against him. He was put to death in 1992. His last words were, "Remember, the death penalty is murder. They (the State of Texas) are taking the life of an innocent man." (Robert Nelson Drew, 1959-1994)

In 1990, I received a letter from Stephen Booker, a poet whose poems appeared in several of the same magazines in which my work was being published. Booker had been on death row for more than two decades. Gwendolyn Brooks and Hayden Carruth, prominent contemporary poets, had also established a personal correspondence with Booker. Booker had reached out to poets who might engage with him in a professional dialogue. Gwendolyn Brooks was his mentor. Booker and I corresponded through the 1990s. Booker had been sentenced to death for murdering and savagely raping an elderly woman. He had confessed to the crime. While awaiting trial in prison, he attacked a guard, so the charge of assault with intent to murder resulted in the additional sentence of ninety-nine years.

Booker was essentially a self-taught poet. He developed his craft while living on death row in solitary confinement. Booker also had an appeal pending. The judge had not allowed certain facts to be presented to the jury during the penalty phase of his trial. After more than twenty years of litigation and legal gymnastics on the part of the prosecution, Booker won the right to a retrial and was to be re-sentenced based on the mitigating evidence previously withheld from the jury. Booker had been beaten and raped by his mother's live-in boyfriend when he was an adolescent. He had run away and had lived on the streets for years. The State of Florida had filed a counter-claim that no procedural error had occurred. After Booker spent years on death row, the Florida Supreme Court ruled that his rights to a fair trial had been violated, and that he had not been adequately represented by the court-appointed public defender. A new trial was ordered for the penalty phase.

In 1998, I was subpoenaed by Booker's new defense council to testify at the new penalty phase of the trial as to Stephen Booker's development as a person/poet in support of the defense claim that Booker was no longer a dangerous person, that he'd become a significant writer with a rehabilitated character. The defense posited the argument that by writing poetry as a professional, Booker had become a more thoughtful, seasoned, responsible man who had developed a sense of self-worth.

As a published poet and college professor teaching Creative Writing and Literature, I was considered an expert witness on the subject of Poetry. I had no standing regarding Booker's emotional or psychological stability. My all-expense-paid whirlwind trip to Florida for the trial included hotel, meals, taxi fares and round-trip transportation from Vermont to Gainesville. I was called to testify, and I did.

The most stunning moment came when the defense attorney asked me, "What is poetry? And what purpose does poetry serve in our society?"

The entire jury leaned forward with fixed interest, anticipating the answer.

***

I met Bruce Burton in 1991. He was teaching Native American Studies at Castleton State College. Both of us taught an early morning class, the only two professors teaching at 8:00 a.m. I poked my head into his office looking for a cup of coffee and introduced myself. He was more than a serious scholar. He was also a committed writer. We formed an immediate bond based on intelligent dialogue and ensuing research projects. Our conversations were insightful and based on our creative investigation into the origins of language, a dialogic of analytical inductions about the primal dimensions of words, alphabets, and imbedded codes that shape human thought. I had spent two years transliterating the Psalms of David using the I-YOU formulation. Burton wrote the introduction for that text:

> For hundreds of years, through oral tradition, from Abraham to the time of Moses, *Parental Agreement* governing *Berith (Bereshet..."In the beginning")* was

the prevailing a priori authority and social imperative. Covenanted to Hebrew "laws," Moses asserted the same authority, vis-à-vis himself as I AM, which meant simply that he was the *Son of a Father (I) and Mother (AM).* This remained the substance and the platform for all subsequent *prophetic* protest and reform, exposing Human Rights violations for centuries into the times of David, a shepherd boy who became a king. Because David was naturally selected and not the progeny from a 'royal' blood line, Saul sought David's death, and for seven years David was hunted and vilified. The mystical notion of *Having Been Chosen By God* was exposed as oxymoronic and false...and those reformers, namely Abraham, Moses, and David were to make evident the false notion that god was the source of corruption...the Temple priests accused and condemned these "upstarts." A protracted social struggle and humanistic revolution ensued, and the same high priests ultimately condemned and executed Jesus (a teacher of the psalms). The priests conspired with their Roman occupiers to thwart human enlightenment while the priests themselves supported despicable and unjust 'laws'. They accused the reformers of the very crimes they were perpetrating. And so, a despotic theocratic patriarchy continued to oppress and suppress the progenitors of a Natural Movement begun 4,000 years ago by earnest and well-intentioned people. And so, consequently, the enslavement, perjuring, and violent persecution of those who followed Abraham is what has come to be called History, a violent tyranny of unjust times. David's psalms (songs) soothed a troubled tyrant and then inspired hundreds and thousands to seek and proclaim their natural rights as a direct connection back to ABBA (The Source of All Legitimate Authority) that is, the man born of a woman (his mother) whom he honors, and a mother who teaches her son to love Humanity.

Burton had also been working on a very sophisticated, complex integrated study, deciphering how intrinsic language codes gave rise to civilization. His book, *The Three D's (Drama, Democracy, and Deity)*, was a monumental chronicle of how religious mythologies emerged and how the evolution of the arts had spawned modern societies. Concepts are encrypted in the words. Subliminally, languages embody the meanings we construct, the laws we institute, and the perversions that have been subconsciously promulgated by hundreds and thousands of years of forgotten knowledge.

I had also been reading other books delving in the origins of language and cultural history, connecting ancient concepts with concrete expressions of existential realities.

Chapter Ten

Feudalism was an economic social-religious construct, where the ultimate power over people and property resided with the "Laird," i.e. the Lord, who provided the loaf (bread), meaning, he owned the land where the wheat was grown. By extension, he possessed all the goods and resources he lorded over. His power and authority was enforced by an army of knights. This was actually an efficient, as well as oppressive, and comprehensive economic system in Europe (circa 1200 A.D).

The Lords delegated authority to squires, and they in turn sought out the craftsmen and skilled workers necessary to produce the goods (pottery, candles, weapons, glass, etc.). Skilled workers, as well as tenants, supplied the services (animal husbandry, cheese-making, crop-growing) required to run the city or the "State." Ultimately, their skills gave rise to the guilds and the merchant-class. Everyone prospered, and those who tilled the land ate the bread of their landlord. No one went hungry or lacked a purpose for their lives. But no one had the freedom to choose otherwise.

The Industrial Revolution brought basic goods to millions and laborers prospered. Hard work matched with ingenuity gave rise to "the middle class." This was the birthing-ground of populist idealism, but at best, economic freedom was limited, with very little social mobility.

Communism asserted the notion that everyone deserved a share of the collective wealth, based on the thesis that all wealth was distributed unjustly. The egregious error of the Marxist manifesto is the assumed notion that the State can justly judge who deserves what share. Marxist-Communist societies, such as existed in Russia and China, were oppressive and unjust and possibly more tyrannical than any monarchy or previous dictatorship in all of human history.

The Technology Revolution brought modern warfare, entertainment, and communications into global reality. Or to be more specific, global realities became dominant, dictating a new prosperity, a democratic wealth based on information and communication at odds with outmoded social, economic, religious, and military realities.

In the 21st Century, we have embarked on a Biogenetic Revolution, which is to usher in a *brave new world* where disease and hunger are apt to be essentially eliminated. Longevity and an endless food supply is the overtly global goal of a world of prosperity in an age of unlimited potential. Simultaneously, we have charted a course toward an absolute totalitarian construct. And those who are rich will be able to afford it.

The sun never sets on purchasing power. Cash is King. Buying and selling money is as profitable as producing goods from raw materials. Countries are selling pollution vouchers. If a country has no pollution, it becomes a surrogate for a country polluting more than its share. Then the average amount of emitted pollution works out to comply with global treaties. Jobs aren't viable security as they once were because workers and owners no longer share in a social contract, so the one seeks to be paid a share of the generated wealth while the corporations seek workers in other countries who have not yet rebelled against being stranded in poverty. Those doing "an honest day's work for an honest day's pay" are dismissed and marginalized by those who control the wealth and resources of an entire global infrastructure. In many countries laborers are still working for "slave" wages (a dollar an hour or less).

In a very real sense, the have-nots do not have the power to change their conditions. A more amorphous tyranny exists in the present materialistic realm. Brazilians living in cardboard houses have color TVs. In the U.S., the condition of poverty is perversely blamed on the poor and, at the same time, accrued wealth has established abundance and ease beyond anything human beings have ever enjoyed in any society.

"Liberalism," which claims to address the problems of lack of productivity and the inability of "the poor" to access equality of rights, services, and the material comforts of this age, ultimately translates into feel-good notions. Planeloads of corn mush and powdered milk are delivered to "starving" people as if to make a real difference, while the idle rich stuff themselves on pheasant and roast beef. The road to hell has been paved with tollbooths. The effect has been the erosion and destabilization of world markets as well as governments. The construct, or "infra-structure," is founded on absolute power and absolute control. Robber-barons and billionaires manipulate and lord over a global economy.

The flow of human history is held hostage. The entire fabric of the world-wide financial system is rife with corrupt bookkeeping, unjust wages, and undemocratic social engineering.

Political demagoguery, rather than honest intellectual debate, has usurped democratic and populist values and supplanted them with a totalitarian worldview. Economic drug wars are one derivative of "policies" that neither work nor attempt to solve the problem.

Illegal markets in cocaine and other drugs has been the cause of political upheaval (on both the right and left) in many "third world" countries. Then, there's the matter of oil, with many countries dealing vast dollar amounts in oil exports on a global scale while shaky political alliances between buyers and sellers adds to animosities and creates more complex instabilities.

The IMF (International Monetary Fund) and the World Bank have attempted to neutralize these destabilizing factors (or at least, counter them) with infusions of cash and work which might offset impoverished norms, especially in countries where many want to work but have no jobs due to backward conditions.

And, poverty in many countries is actually controlled and institutionalized. In Egypt, for example, some people move to the Cairo dump as an upwardly mobile opportunity, in order to live better than they might if they had a job in the city. A pack of cigarettes in Poland costs twenty dollars. In the U.S., gasoline is so expensive that low-income earners are forced to use much of their disposable income to commute to their jobs. A gallon of spring water is also very expensive.

At the same time, Saudi Arabia remains a feudal state. Old ideas and stable realities, which controlled prices and established order, were overridden by greed-driven policies. After hundreds of years of living securely (if not more simply) because supply and demand created a fair market, all bets are off. Those values no longer hold sway. Obsessive materialism drives pollution. Global warming and dwindling rain forests are two byproducts of the modern age.

From a historical standpoint, the War against Humanity escalated in the middle of the 20th Century. World War II established an infrastructure of industrialized mass-murder. I'm not referring only to what the Nazis did, but to the "war machine" that all nations were willing to embrace. Billions of dollars has been spent for bombs, airplanes, submarines, missiles, land mines, and nuclear weapons.

For thousands of years, wars, bloody as they were, and battles, were confined to one army pitted against another. But somewhere along the way, a distinct change occurred. War became the slaughter of thousands upon thousands of innocent civilians, mainly mothers, children, and old people whose only offence was being in the path of a battle plan. The deaths of the millions of innocent people falls squarely on those who condone war, excuse war, and support war. Those who did nothing or do nothing or give no voice against this systematic slaughter of innocent human beings are complicit perpetrators of Evil. The nightmare and horror of manufactured Evil (also known as "War") continues at an ever-alarming pace. Human lives pass through the eternal veil very quickly, but institutions and corporations live on in their industrial agendas.

Don't go down to silence! Get off your couch, turn off the television and get busy putting an end to this monstrous world system, which manufactures evil for the purpose of profiting from the deaths of innocent people.

***

An anthropologist ran with some Bushmen in Africa for almost six months. In that time he wowed his hosts with "wonders," including lighting the fire at night with matches. When he was leaving to return home, he offered the matches to the chief, who quickly refused them. When the chief's son sought to take them, the chief chastised him.

The anthropologist asked the chief what his objection was. After all, the chief had allowed the use of matches all during his stay with them.

The chief explained that it was one thing to be hospitable, but another to allow the corrupt to replace the pure, because making fire with flint cost his people nothing, neither morally nor spiritually. The chief naturally mistrusted an outside influence, which might take control away from his people and put it into the hands of "invisible strangers."

The 20th Century burgeoned with inventions and innovations that changed human life at the grass roots forever and inexorably—the airplane, the telephone, the computer, the car, electric appliances, motion pictures, elevators, and swimming pools. Of course, there were other inventions that caused great harm.

In the 20th Century, we were taught that the dinosaurs died out because they were dumb (i.e. stupid). They were big but they had little brains. They were real good at eating but not at determining their own destiny. They lived in a "dino eat dino" world. They didn't invent anything. They didn't even try to promote a safe environment for their offspring to grow up in. And they didn't seem to evolve into smarter, more survivable creatures. They very well may have been made extinct by rodents eating dinosaur eggs, which were left unprotected in open nests of sand (merely a poetic speculation).

Two brontosauruses were munching in the forest. One turns to the other and says: "Wow, look at that. Peas the size of brains!"

We know only what we believe. We believe only that which we choose to believe. In our most lucid times as intelligent beings, we employ our experience and knowledge to bring us beyond what prevents us from making true progress.

When we focus our talents and genius, we solve the human problems we contend with every day. I know nothing of how to generate electricity, but I am completely empowered to turn on the lights.

Chapter Eleven

In the early 1950s, we were taught how to respond to the air raid siren. Air raid drills were meant to get us used to the idea that a nuclear war was not only a real possibility, but was also an imminent threat. The blaring horn would sound at any time, similar to a fire alarm. We were taught not to go outside, but to remain at our desks and in our room. We were to crouch under our desks, covering our eyes and face, thus protecting us from the glare of a nuclear flash and also from the shattering glass and other elements of the conflagration we would be prepared to experience—in the event it was not a drill.

In this way, we were shown how to spend our last moments on Earth, huddled alone under our desks like trapped rodents, with only enough time to say good-bye to ourselves.

Albert Einstein was bluntly asked what World War III would be like, now that we had nuclear weapons. "I can't say for sure," he replied. "But I can tell you with certainty what World War IV will be like."

"How's that?" the reporter asked.

"Men will fight World War IV with sticks and stones," Einstein mused. "After World War III, mankind will find himself back in the Stone Age."

Pierre Boulle's novel, *Planet of the Apes,* was made into a very significant film in 1967, about a planet where apes have human personalities and the "humans" are more like dumb, docile simpletons. Enter three astronauts who crash there after a long voyage in their spacecraft. The main character unravels the secret of the "madhouse" he finds himself in only at the very end of the movie, when he realizes he has crashed on planet Earth some two thousand years into the future, after a nuclear world war destroyed human civilization and mutated apes into sapient beings.

Most haunting is the ape doctor's observation, "Beware of Man, for he alone kills for sport." The last image is truly a classic moment in film-making, stunning in its visual presentation, when we see what's left of the Statue of Liberty, in ruins on the shoreline. The hero falls to his knees, pounding the sand, declaring, "You finally did it! " The nucleation of the human race is revealed.

The introduction of television into the American home in the 1950s was hailed as a monumental accomplishment, advancing the human desire to communicate both verbally and visually in a meaningful networking of human endeavor. It was seen as a great invention, *a tool for education.* Generally speaking, television was accepted as a friendly feature of a better life. Oh, there were a few eggheads who called it "a vast wasteland" or a "one-eyed monster," but for the most part, everyone put a TV in their living room and the whole family sat down and watched *I Love Lucy* with hypnotic delight. During the commercial break, we were treated to packages of cigarettes with very pretty legs, dancing in a chorus line.

And so began the dumbing down of Americans. TV did bring some innovative changes and ideas into the 20th Century mix, but for the most part, it was—and still is—the single most identifiable destructive force in the social and intellectual development of the human race, second only to modern warfare in its devastating effect on civilization and culture. Whatever good television might have potentially offered at its inception, we can rightly conclude after more than a half-century of broadcast programming, that it is an enemy of creative thought.

Television stifles and stunts the imaginative mind, and wields a destructive power to devalue information. TV is a cesspool of pseudo-intellectual and anti-intellectual propaganda. Its ultimate appeal is to the lowest common denominator—a vision of a flat-screen world, a commercial boondoggle undermining human development while promoting unimaginative, violent, and stupid ideas.

One should not take too much solace in the fact that one is free to watch or not watch. The genie was let out of the bottle a long time ago. The damage to children and the intellectual malaise TV brought forth has been inculcated into the very psyche of modern society, especially in young, impressionable children. The evil that men do lives after them. That explains why they have reruns.

In his novel *1984*, Orwell warned of a future where you don't watch television. It watches you. But he missed the worst and more dangerous aspect of the coming age. You waste your life, your precious time, allowing your thoughts to be sculpted by television. What we learn is how to be mesmerized without engaging our creative imaginations, and the agenda for our experience is dictated by illusions, subterfuge, and lies. You become alienated from others. You lose the ability to distinguish art as form. The viewer trades the nuances of aesthetics for a one-dimensional cycloptic IT, a perpetual state of non-being, where one is transformed into a passive spectator willingly deceived into submission and silence. And when IT says YOU, IT means YOU is IT.

The TV news anchor says, "See you here tomorrow," but what they are really saying is "See me on TV tomorrow." The news anchor does not see you, does not know you, and does not speak words of relationship to real people.

The monolithic control of information is one of the pejorative tools that enable the structures of government to perpetuate totalitarian constructs. People are being intimidated to keep silent, and they are discouraged from actively trying to make a significant difference to control their own lives in relation to the real power exerted to manipulate and manufacture public opinion (i.e. IT-consciousness). Human rights are being negated. Populations are being divided by contrived social "issues," while prejudices and stereotypes are re-enforced.

In 2005, reports filtered into the U.S. news that there are secret prisons in Siberia and Thailand maintained by the C.I.A., where prisoners have no rights and due process has simply been eliminated. Clearly, this is not in keeping with "justice for all," nor recognized as a legal practice. Habeas corpus is ignored. And the President has the authority to order the assassination of American citizens. But somehow it has been accepted as necessary and "good." We are no longer innocent until proven guilty.

Politicians and legislators in government and think tanks are co-opted to serve the will of corporations who finance their campaigns and agendas. Citizens are less able (or willing) to speak out or legislate to produce a just society. We know, by our own experience, in ways we can see, the erosion process is already rampant and social contracts no longer work to see the nation prosper from the bottom up.

According to Jane Jacobs, in her book DARK AGE AHEAD, "Mankind is headed for a self-destructive dead end."

From Shakespeare to Joseph Heller and William Golding, with Hemmingway in between, no piece of writing typified the 20th Century post-World War mindset more than Heller's *Catch 22*. It was the ultimate absurdist statement, which exposed that reality was only reality because we all agree what we say it is. Or, in its most basic form, you can only see me when I'm not here. When I'm here, I'm not here, so you can't see me.

Catch 22 exposed bureaucracy and red tape and war itself as an insane enterprise. *King of Hearts* makes the same statement. Sane people are quite insane, or more correctly, "sane society" is absurdly not sane. Insane people, those who are disconnected from the irrational and violent "normal" world, are really the only sane people. The phrase "catch 22" became a well-recognized coded message for anyone who had come to know that we had met the enemy and had come to realize that "the enemy" is a web of tyranny shrouded in absurdity. Milo, in Heller's book, had figured out how to send American bombers to bomb the Americans for the Nazis (for a significant sum of money).

The message of modern times, typified in modern warfare, is that life is an insane experience. And, as Erich Fromm said, "You have to be insane in order to survive in an insane world."

Chapter Twelve

It was James Cagney, as the sociopath Arthur Cody Jarrett in Raoul Walsh's *White Heat* (written by Virginia Kellog), who stood atop the hydrogen tower at the end of the flick, surrounded by a SWAT Team. Cody is determined to shoot it out, with no intention of being taken alive. The SWAT Team, unable to restrain or capture him, unleashes a storm of bullets. He's blown up in a mushroom cloud, consumed in a raging conflagration, proclaiming his ultimate victory.

The final image is an obvious and potent reference to the ominous age in which Man creates and perpetrates his own final demise. The ending is more than just another memorable moment from a movie—it's the absolute finalé for Mankind, and it reveals the fatal flaw imbedded in every man. James Cagney, in his signature "tough guy" splendor, mad as any lunatic who ever walked on the Earth, takes great delight in making his last stand against the furies. With no fear of death to restrain him, his psychotic personality looms as large as any

Shakespearean villain (cast in the mold of Richard III). His character takes a perverse pleasure in his own destruction. He has spent his miscreant life celebrating mayhem and a perverse pleasure humiliating others. Of course, we don't want to be like him. We are very much repulsed by him. We don't want to be destroyed with him either. But he's like a suicide bomber or rather, more accurately, a homicidal maniac. So there he is, atop the hydrogen plant, on the tower, blown up in a mushroom cloud, proclaiming (with delight and fire in his eyes), "Made it, Ma! Top of the world!"

Spiritually, there is incompetence, inflexibility, and a lack of integrity that is growing in all areas of human endeavor. Not so long ago, a space shuttle disintegrated on reentry into the Earth's atmosphere because of a miniscule pin-hole in its hull (probably the result of shoddy workmanship and poor maintenance). Many parents fret for their children being in public schools because many of these schools foster and promote slovenly practices. It is often the case that parents and children are no longer in direct communication. The students who perpetrated the Columbine massacre planned their evil act of terrorism right under the noses of their parents, buying guns on the Internet while keeping computer diaries of what they were planning.

Selfishness and personal destruction are woven into an insane inhumanity and glorified in many movies. Hatred of other human beings becomes a reflection of abject selfishness because a person ultimately comes to believe that what they think and believe is so much more important and good than what someone else believes, and that anything they do is justified by the cause they serve. Terrorists promote fear and perpetrate violence to enforce their opinions and their beliefs.

Chapter Thirteen

Ordinary people are living in fear that senseless acts of violence might occur at any time, in any place. People live in spiritual fear because their finite self-lives are dwarfed by a global omnisphere that reinforces isolation and alienation in a meaningless secular society. Terrorists prey upon civilians who are conveniently targeted specifically because they are defenseless. Terrorist acts of violence fuels a xenophobic mentality that permeates society and further propels small-mindedness into the darkness (spiritually and socially). Fear and loathing has established a tyranny in our midst.

What passes for peace in the world collectively, even as the times result in a more fearful state of being, is, in the balance, promulgating more tyrannical nation-states that disregard human truths and realities. Humanitarian goals are buried with the innocent dead.

Anna Eleanor Roosevelt, author, mother, humanitarian, born into the wealthy Roosevelt family, married her second cousin, Franklin. She was the favored niece of Theodore, and a significant role model in my up-bringing. She belonged to a family of inherited wealth, who took seriously the notion that they were privileged to be part of the "enlightened rich." She was an educated woman who chose to bear the burden of her position to speak for those less fortunate. She dedicated her entire life to what she believed, and she lived to see her beliefs have a real impact on society and humanity.

She was First Lady from 1932 to 1945. She put all the prestige her position allowed to bring about civil rights and an end to segregation. She believed government should work as the defender of the helpless. She loved humanity. She was sweet, kind, and caring. She worked tirelessly for social justice. She lived to see Civil Rights become the law of the land.

Her determination to see world peace become a reality motivated her to single-handedly advocate for a world organization dedicated to peace, and ultimately coerced the leaders of all the nations, when World War II ended, to create the United Nations.

After weeks of meeting and negotiating, the leaders were prepared to go home and quibble endlessly about what kind of organization they should create. She embarrassed them, applied moral pressure, appealed to their better nature, and indicted their cowardly consciences, so that they dared not walk away without putting together some kind of world organization dedicated to peace, that would somehow work to prevent future slaughters and holocausts. Finally, they all signed the United Nations Charter (1948).

In 1962, she drafted and wrote the thirty articles of the Declaration of Human Rights. She tirelessly waged a monumental campaign to see it adopted by the U.N. as a standard of law and decency for all humanity, expressing a spiritual connectedness to a harmonious universe. World War II had brought chaos, evil, and depravity to millions, and reveals a history of indifference by those who ignore the suffering of others.

High Sierra is a wispy and sentimental existentialist 1941 movie with a haunting poetic essence. The film was directed by Raoul Walsh and produced by John Huston. Humphrey Bogart is "Mad Dog" Roy Earle, an ex-con and robber on the run. He is a tragic, definable "anti-hero," conflicted within himself, an outlaw, but not an evil man. Earle commits acts of humane kindness as he flees from authorities. He befriends a poor family, using a sizeable chunk of his robbery money to pay for a young woman's operation to repair her clubfoot. He rescues another woman (played by Ida Lupino) who has been deserted in a small town, penniless and without a friend. She falls in love with him, but he isolates her from his ignoble criminal past. When he's spotted by the police in the shadow of the Sierras, he leaves her behind. In an operatic and thrilling car chase with police, Earle races to a dead end, high up in the mountains. There, he climbs to a ledge to make his last stand. The film is a haunting reminder that Man, out of harmony with Nature, finds no peace in his "fallen" state. To the very end,

Earle seems likeable, noble, human, and laced with decency, a Promethean *everyman,* trapped and alone, with no way out of his impending death. The mountains provide an epical backdrop for the finale. In spite of his flawed life, he preserves his human dignity even as he is gunned down by the police.

Chapter Fourteen

Scientists have formulated and calculated the odds that life of any kind can exist, one to the minus thirteenth power, or .0000000000001, which is the mathematical chance that life exists. For a one-celled animal to spring to life—"life" being defined as "a self-sustaining organism able to reproduce itself"—two hundred separate but absolutely in specific order chemical events must occur. Also, this does not account for, nor explain, where the material itself originates from, which is a completely separate but formidable question.

Leaving these in the background let us consider that our limited, but generally sane, observation is that inert matter doesn't spontaneously transform into living organisms. Moreover, we can rightly deduce that without the spontaneous spark of life, also mysteriously present, no life will arise. Thus, one to the minus thirteenth power expresses the impossibility for life to exist as we comprehend the enigma of consciousness. Scientists can neither duplicate nor explain why we are who we are, confounding even the most brilliant astrophysicists and biochemists who are paid many thousands of dollars to consider and investigate the human phenomenon.

Carl Sagan, noted scientist and astronomer, put it this way: If you were blindfolded and standing in Yankee Stadium with three darts in your hand, and you knew that somewhere in the stadium was a balloon floating, you would have three chances to break the balloon without taking the blindfold off. Bursting the balloon would create life. The odds of hitting the balloon approximate the opportunity for life to exist in our present condition. How life began is a "long, intractable problem," according to Dr. George Cody of the Carnegie Institute. Whether you believe in the Big Bang Theory or The Citric Acid Cycle Theory or The Hot Metallic Theory or even Kaku's Theory of Everything, these fashionable and accepted biological notions ultimately start from the idea that life began spontaneously from lesser non-living materials. Even when a specific scientific explanation can show all the materials present to make a particular theory believable, it is never possible, in any objective way, to explain or duplicate why non-living matter assembles into living cells.

Dr. Gunther Websterhauser has suggested "the iron-sulfur world" theory, which states that metallic conversion of carbon-oxide eats through metal into a two-compound chemical capable of transforming electrons within enzymes. Pursuing this theory with a grant for 40 million dollars, Dr. Websterhauser performed eight sequential lab steps, which are required to generate a "lipid" (a fatty chemical, which bubbles around a living cell and keeps the DNA embodied within it). But, when the man-made lipids were introduced into a dish containing the very cells lipids are created to function with, they would not spontaneously surround the cells but simply remained inert.

The Broth Theory argues that the conditions of the cosmic stew cannot be duplicated or even comprehended fully because there are too many variable and complex conditions required, and they all have to be happening together at the same time to make life a scientific reality (which happened over an incomprehensible time span).

One overriding message, though, is that human beings exist at the end of a long, unconscious chemical chain of cosmic dust. The Chaos Theory goes so far as to state that all life is meaningless and bent toward self-destruction, or, as stated in the more neutral concept of entropy, the tendency of all matter is to breakdown and come apart.

The Theory of Continuous Creation (although more beneficent in recognizing life as a positive development) suggests that after billions of years forming galaxies out of the cosmic dust, the only long-term purpose is that all the energy will be sucked back in, collapsing on itself and will be reduced to non-conscious light particles (essentially intimating a scientific nihilism). These constructs have been a constant cosmological frame of reference in my thought-world. These notions have become embedded in my psyche, as points of reference.

My poetry seeks identity in the search for meaning and finds security in the poems (or, what could be for some, a lack of identity and a source of insecurity).

In the Dark Ages, people sought and found meaning in a flat-earth cosmology. The great cathedrals of Catholicism in the Middle Ages reflected an absolute belief in a sky-god who had created the earth at the center of his creation, and everyone who believed, thought the world was flat. The sun "rose and set." The Bible specifically stated that as fact.

After centuries of intellectual and scientific censorship, a newfound reality emerged—learning through scientific experimentation and discovery, which gave rise to books and scholarship. Universities were established and an Age of Enlightenment and Reason followed. In the 20th Century, people went to the movies, read newspapers, used telephones, watched television, and traveled across the global world. Ultimately, we came to believe that our ascent via technology had separated us utterly from nature and our human identity.

And, in extreme, perverse manifestations, we see how a person can be formed in their character and then function as a social being or an anti-social being, connected as a healthy participant or disconnected from reality and capable of atrocities while seeming to live a "normal" life at the same time. Modern society produces disassociated personalities who are capable of gunning down innocent people. Or, in order to satisfy a need to avenge some greater wrong, they believe they are justified in perpetrating violence to rectify their existential insecurities. Some of these miscreants become known as "mass murderers" or stalkers or serial killers. In effect, these social misfits are psychopathic manipulators of a poisoned view of the world, in which evil deeds count as much toward self-worth as good deeds might to a more normal, healthy, well-adjusted person.

Chapter Fifteen

The Big Bang and Chaos Theories are nothing more than absurdist poetic notions which depersonalize real human values, nor do these theories give inspirational rise to intellectual curiosity. What motivates us to behave well? Why seek to have an objective discussion of what is known and what is not known? In a material world of infinite expanse and eternal notions lodged in time, Albert Einstein's concept of time and space is the most plausible scientific theory. His reckoning may well be as close to the truth as anyone can ever know. He concluded that infinitely falling light particles have formed all of what we are and what we experience. Time and space are relative to our perception of these cosmic events. Or, at least, that was the prevailing perception in the 20th Century, when an orderly and definable universe seemed within our grasp.

I went to Canada, traveling through the maritime provinces in 1967, and I saw how the financial support of the Canadian government allowed artists a much more a meaningful voice in their society. Artists, poets included, were given much more credibility and their value to society seemed more appreciated and acknowledged. I also traveled to Mexico City in 1969, Jamaica (twice), and I saw firsthand what real poverty looks like. I lived in Italy in 1972, where history and art created an atmosphere of inspired thought. I had a life-changing experience studying Michelangelo's depictions in the Sistine Chapel. I spent time at the Uffizi and was inspired to awe by the paintings of Van Gogh. Culmination for me and validation for my work followed when I was awarded The Leonardo Da Vinci Cultural Achievement Award in Florence in 1976.

In England and Scotland, I was received as a respected voice connected to a long history of literary accomplishment. My books of poetry were in the libraries at the University of Edinburgh and The Bodleian Library at Oxford. I toured Switzerland, where sanity and peace seemed institutional. In Israel, I stood on the shores of the Kinneret (the Sea of Galilee), toured the ruins of Caesarea, and lived in the suburbs of Jerusalem. I was received as a poet of distinction at Mt. Scopus, where *The Stonecutters at War With the Cliff Dwellers* was hailed as a major cultural and artistic accomplishment.

For more than four decades, I devoted myself to writing poems, pursuing the Tao, and perceiving the infinite by the definitive finite. I regard the poem as an act of will, a creative expression of form and meaning. I dedicated myself to the work of writing and producing poems, the caveat being that you can work hard, write an endless number of poems, and end up with nothing that matters, with a product that does not achieve the intended impact, nor would be valued as art.

In 1976, I spent a semester working in concert with Howard Ehrenfeld, photographer and conceptual artist. Our unique freewheeling association and friendship sprang from my days at Clark University where we first met. We presented a seminar in Baltimore on the concept of uncontaminated works—art that does not succumb to sentimentality nor rely on classical form. Of course, the artist must self-declare a process which is ultimately communicated by the work, and no intellectual explanation can supplant that reality. The experience with the work is what reveals its essential nature. Artists are not innocent bystanders.

My books were commercially finding markets in Boston, Washington D.C., New York City, Chicago, Iowa City, Omaha, Boulder, San Francisco and Berkeley. In the spirit of Walt Whitman's legacy, I hitchhiked across the United States from New York City to San Francisco, giving poetry readings, selling my hand-made books and Four Zoas publications, as well as working with other bookmakers and printers along the way.

I established myself as a writer and published poet. I'd been a small press editor and publisher. I'd received a record number of five grants from the N.E.A., several more from C.O.S.M.E.P. *The Four Zoas Journal* had been acknowledged by the *Library Journal* as "a beautiful magazine with an important mission." I'd owned fifty acres in Massachusetts on the backside of the Quabbin Reservoir, and I'd lived in the woods. I lived the life of a full-time writer, in itself, an accomplishment of some distinction (in my own mind). I had created my own destiny and fulfilled my ambitions.

But I was haunted more than ever by the persistent notion that I had failed to attain my place on the great Mandela, whatever that might be. It was not so much a matter of establishing new goals as creating a path of personal growth, equanimity, and ease. I envisioned an intrinsic development, organic, as well as human, to enhance my way forward. I had no modus vivendi, no analytic or esoteric means to cope with what loomed large in my psyche. I was facing an impasse without a definable pathway to what might come next.

I was thirty-two years old in 1977. I was still a seeker yearning for a more complete and positive vision of my human identity and a definitive meaning by enhanced perception and introspection. I sought a state of heightened awareness. I knew the drug culture was merely an escape from being connected to pure being, something that became especially clear to me after I had experienced a number of LSD trips.

I concluded that such drugs were debilitating and only diminished human capacity and capability. Whatever I had gained from the experience of expanded consciousness was obscured by the persistent realization that the quality of my writing during that same period of time was inexcusably poor. I destroyed something in the order of two hundred pages of poems and an entire novel as I was convinced that what I wrote under the influence of "mind-expanding drugs" did not represent my creative abilities or meet the objective standards of excellence I wanted to attain.

I visited the New England Institute for Personal Growth and Human Development with the clear ambition to "rediscover" myself. I studied and practiced Transactional Analysis with Dr. Ed Gurwitz for two years. Feldenkrais with Josef DelaGrotte. Gestalt and Psychotherapy with Jack Canfield. I was enlightened and liberated by Eric Berne's monumental book *Transactional Analysis*, which provided the structure for understanding complex human motivation. Claude Steiner's *Games People Play* defined the intricate web of scripted behaviors with devastating clarity. I was provoked and challenged to seek and find the pure Being that my poetry had always voiced.

In my academic career, I had studied the writings of the first "modern" writer, William Shakespeare, modern because he explored the tragic consequences of flawed personal (psychological) exigencies. Hamlet's noble intentions visit dreadful results on those he loved. King Lear's fall from absolute power is self-inflicted by his unchecked self-importance and shortsightedness. Julius Caesar's personal ambition and disregard for Roman law provokes his fellow members of the Senate to assassinate him. Othello succumbs to jealousy and violence because he believes the lies of an evil adversary, and strangles his wife.

William Blake created his own mythology (*The Four Zoas*) to challenge the established mythology and cosmology of the Bible. Blake embraced reason and science as the antidote for human ignorance and mythical religious belief systems.

In *The Marriage of Heaven and Hell*, his poetic treatise on Being and Meaning, Blake set forth his abiding notions that "Energy can neither be created or destroyed" and that "Energy is eternal delight."

Aldous Huxley, author of *Brave New World, Ape and Essence,* and *Island* and William Golding's *Lord of the Flies* portray a deterministic universe in which human flaws are organic and genetic, that self-alienation, combined with self-inflicted destructive economic and social forces, results in dire consequences for civilization.

Robinson Jeffers, a poet whose existential notions portray the forces of Nature coalescing with the destructive capacity of the human psyche. He narrates a poetic mirror, which reflects the perverse, unchecked passions of sexual desire, cruel motives, and the sub-conscience workings of the mind. The Nazi industrial war machine, the death camps, the advent of the Atom Bomb, and the ensuing arms race confirmed that human survival was at risk because human beings have perversely used Nature to pervert natural law.

So, I was determined to explore how new age psychology and classical literary allegories could be worked together to envision a modern allegorical narrative of the two polarities of the human condition—our humanity redefined by our hopes and dreams (i.e. the imaginative) on one end of the

154

spectrum and, in contrast, the brutality, insanity, insensitivity, and manic behaviors of a flawed human nature.

My task, as writer, was to comprehend the causes of violence and cruelty when juxtaposed to the known consequences of miscreant beings choosing to be self-destructive.

"Hell is the Truth, discovered too late."

Chapter Sixteen

No news story reverberated more with evil intent and senseless violence than the sacrificial stabbing murder of actress Sharon Tate and her unborn baby by Charles Manson's "family."

Manson and his "followers" brutally murdered four Hollywood socialites in one night, and the crime was sensationalized, in that Manson, a charismatic cult leader, had brainwashed his lackeys to do the deed. Manson wasn't with them but had sent them on their mission. In court, he presented a chilling diatribe (his testimony on the stand) of his self-justified, cold-hearted view of the world. He became a symbolic embodiment of a social misfit and sociopath who saw no distinction between criminals and righteous people.

What is most disturbing is the fact that Manson's miscreant personality is a cultivated by-product of the American Dream. Two of the most sensational news stories of the 20th Century are very troubling to anyone concerned with knowing "the truth," because disinformation and use of the media to engineer public sentiment had already been successfully instituted in the 1960s, with the

Kennedy assassination, the Vietnam War, and a host of other "known untruths" reported in print and on television as fact. First, was the Jonestown Massacre, where more than nine hundred people, including many children, were murdered in the utopian *People's Temple* community in Guyana, South America. They had followed Rev. Jim Jones. They were seeking salvation.

One rumor stated that Jones was funneling millions of dollars from his supporters into left wing revolutions in South America, so the C.I.A. arranged for him to be taken out. One cover story or rumor was the "disinformation" that Jones was working for the C.I.A. and had established Jonestown under Operation MK/ULTRA, so the government could experiment with mind control, brainwashing, and social engineering. Somehow, the operation was either botched or amplified to include the mass murder suicide of everyone living in Jonestown. Some were shot. The rest supposedly drank "cool aide" laced with poison. Congressman Leo Ryan was gunned down as he tried to leave, and Jim Jones was found with a bullet in his brain, supposedly killed in a suicide pact with one of his bodyguards.

The case against Wayne Williams seemed to be engineered by the news media. In 1979, there was a rash of murders of black children in Atlanta, Georgia. The evidence against Williams seemed scanty at best. But, Williams was portrayed by the media to the public as "guilty" beyond a shadow of a doubt, well before he actually went to trial.

Hysteria gripped the city and the nation. Several plausible rumors were circulating. One, that an active Satanic underground network was kidnapping children and sacrificing them. Or, two, that the Klu Klux Klan was murdering the children as part of an on-going race war, hoping to destabilize the black community in an effort to undo the effects of civil rights (which had made integration a normal feature of American life). Certainly, in the aftermath of Martin Luther King's murder, many people believed (and still do) that James Earle Ray was an F.B.I. hireling. It should be emphasized that Ray never stood trial and the facts of his case have never been presented in open court.

Wayne Williams was ultimately charged with only two murders, but he was blamed for all 27 deaths of the children in the Atlanta area. His motive, according to the press, was that he was a homosexual who hated himself and hated being a Black man. They claimed that in his twisted mind, he killed the children because he desired them and by killing them, he would prevent them from turning out like him.

There was only one "eyewitness," a policeman, and only his testimony linked Williams to any of the crime scenes. Supposedly, he had caught a glimpse of Wayne's car speeding away from a bridge where a child's body was later found. Otherwise, the only evidence against Williams was a few hairs and fibers found on a rug used to wrap up one of the bodies. The evidence against Williams wasn't convincing, but the press made the case sound ironclad. Williams was found guilty.

Williams is serving a life sentence. All attempts by his family to get him a new trial based on evidence never heard have been denied as recently as the late 1990s.

The case of "Son of Sam" (David Berkowitz) is especially sensational. In many ways, his particulars are not much different than other psychopaths or serial killers. He roamed the streets of Brooklyn at odd times and off hours murdering "victims" at random. After a stint in the army (stationed in Korea), he had been a cab driver and a hardware clerk. He was a miscreant "loner" who had been a pyromaniac and had spent much of his childhood torturing small animals. He blended in. He was not flamboyant or outwardly weird or even very outspoken in his views. Every once in a while, he walked the streets at night and shot someone and killed them. Obviously, he felt a surge of power when he went out on these "hunts." Leading an otherwise insignificant existence and even seeing himself as a "nobody," these random acts of violence made him a "somebody." He terrorized New York City (1999). He killed eleven people. When he was finally caught, he was found guilty and sentenced to six life terms. He claimed and presented in court as his motive for the killings that the Devil, speaking to him directly, had told him what to do. And how had the Devil spoken to him? Through a dog. Maybe his defense was the truth. He may very well have been an insane sociopath. It would seem from all the accounts that he had indeed received instructions from his dog.

Chapter Seventeen

1999. A memorable venue. I was signed to give
a significant poetry reading at a local Massachusetts
college to be held in a new art complex and gallery.
The hall was a three-story cathedral with prestigious
oil paintings hung in ominous repose. There was
almost no advertising for my reading and no liberal
arts students were informed, invited, or required to
attend. Fifty chairs were set up at one end of the
hall. Eight people formed the audience. But my
performance was the same as if eighty or eight
hundred people were there. I was also being paid a
sizeable stipend. Of course, I would have enjoyed
the venue more if there had been a better turnout,
but I read my poetry and sang original songs with as
much intensity as I would for a packed house.

The audience of eight included an English
professor, several students, two members of the
museum staff, and Joe Bernstein, Director of
Communications for the college. Joe was the former
Director of the News Bureau at NBC.

After the reading, Joe introduced himself. He told me that he was very impressed with my presentation and asked me to join him for a late lunch in the VIP dining room. He suggested that there might be another gig for me, an opportunity that would be quite unique (if not challenging).

Joe put together a special program sponsored by the college, to bring gifted young high school writers to a daylong workshop conference. Students headed for a career in broadcasting were sponsored by their schools to attend the conference, accompanied by their English teachers. Many of these students would be offered internships as a result of their participation. Workshops were headed up by high-powered media personalities from 60 Minutes, ESPN, and The New York Times, among other notable and venerated media outlets. A keynote speaker with star status kicked off the daylong event.

Joe suggested that I could be the poet-in-residence, conduct workshops and talk about how young writers could advance their desires to get published. Joe envisioned me as "the wild card" in the program. He was taking a risk that poetry would be of interest to students, as all workshops were elected individually by the students. There was no guarantee that poetry workshops would be an attractive draw, but Joe was impressed enough with my work to give me a slot.

I held three workshops packed with young poets eager to enhance their writing skills and learn what essentials were required to delve into the substantive ideas that make for poetic language. And many came to the one workshop that focused on how to get published. There were also quite a few English teachers who sat in on the sessions (advisors to the students serving as chaperones for the daylong event). They were hoping to gain insights on how to teach poetry in their classrooms. In reality, many high school English teachers really don't comprehend the value of poetry nor are they educated to why poetry is a substantive art form that speaks to the depth of one's being.

Joe stopped by for a few minutes during one of the sessions. When he saw that I had a room full of students intensely involved with my curriculum, he was very gratified, so much so that he offered me a place in the next round of workshops to be held the following year. I was part of Joe's "team" of resident professionals for the ensuing six years and presented poetry workshops to hundreds of young writers. Joe retired in 2007. I wasn't kept in the mix once he was gone, and I appreciated his support for my abilities and professional skill. I admired him as well for his undaunted commitment to include me to represent poetry in that venue. He was a gutsy man of definite cultural standards, an ally to the arts, an astute risk-taker, and a magnanimous friend.

That same year, I had taken a year off from teaching and was writing poems with a renewed sense of purpose. I submitted a few of my most recent poems to the *Chinese International Poetry Magazine.* My writings were published in China. In one issue, I was the featured poet. With a circulation of eighty thousand, the quarterly invigorated me to keep submitting my poems to a number of prestigious publications. At the same time, I maintained a rigorous schedule reading my poetry and performing my songs at various venues.

Chapter Eighteen

All of us find ourselves in a confusing world of stark contradictions, where lives can be lost any time, in any situation. Being human is a precarious circumstance. Stress is a normal feature of real life. So, solving problems, overcoming overwhelming resistance, and living as a fully evolved human being requires active decision-making and action based on making sane choices. Victims and persecutors are perverse roles in a perverse game. Human beings live in the eternal moment, "now," and destiny is derived from being connected to the choices that shape one's life.

When you boil down the whole LIFE EXPERIENCE to the essential ingredients, strictly from a spiritual perspective, there are these two absolutes: First, if you fear LIFE you will waste your opportunity to live and you will never know the glory or the joy of real fulfillment. And second, if you do not use your time wisely or fail to value your precious time, then you will miss your opportunity to live fully. I was focused on one thing. And I had no time to waste or misspend.

After a lifetime of living to gain wisdom, I have neither regrets nor misgivings about the brief life we actually do have to strive for and achieve what we want. For those who live a life of purpose, there is a discernible destiny in what we do. We are not victims. We take responsibility for our choices.

The aberrations speak for themselves. Who more than Elvis became a sorry and macabre version of himself? He loved the myth of himself more than the truth he might have embraced. He believed the lie that "Elvis" was real. He was addicted to the image. The gaudy costumes. The adulation of screaming fans. The wealth and money he accrued seemed to have no purpose other than to flaunt his success. The substance of the man just didn't match up with the image. It's bad enough to con the public with a fantasy. It's quite another when you believe it yourself to your own destruction.

Stewart Granger was quite old when a woman walked up to him at a train station and asked, "Did you used to be Stewart Granger?"

"Yes," he replied, both amused and honored that she remembered him. "I used to be Stewart Granger."

At 40, Elvis could have directed his life toward any number of positive pursuits. He was rich, affable, a man of immense fame with a legendary influence on the popular culture. To this day, deceased, he's the best selling recorded solo artist. But instead, he frantically lost himself in drugs, isolation, and perverse efforts to reclaim his former status as a god-like icon of the 20th Century. He ended his career and his life trapped in a pathetic caricature of what he had once been (a legend without a life, with no substance of character or inner worth to back up the illusion).

A.S. Neil, in his book *Summerhill*, suggests that well-adjusted people are not necessarily driven to be financially successful nor do they strive to be "great" movers and shakers. Neil set up his private school in England to teach his students to be responsible, diligent, and thorough. He designed an open-ended curriculum within which students were free to study (or not) whatever subjects they chose. What he did insist upon was that their habits would reflect their sincerity of purpose, and then, from that, they would learn to be aware human beings, capable of ruling over their own lives. Neil's goal was to encourage learning and to instill character in his students.

What causes us to seek revolution of spirit and mind? Changing the construct requires a great deal of effort, physical and psychological. Music, art, politics, sports, religious beliefs, love of food, money, and raw power are all reflections of inspired thought.

But what does all that inspire us to do? Our loyalty ought not be blind obedience to "what works." We must also be fundamentally willing to be risk takers and innovative seekers. We acknowledge those who dedicated themselves to doing so. We ought to be embracing meaningful change, not frustrating those who are seeking the solutions. "High performance" values are stressful. Jobs become obsolete and things wear out. They outlive their usefulness.

But there are sustaining elements that give life meaning which do not become time-weary nor apt to fade because their potency is only good for when they are employed or popular. A university education was touted as necessary for a high-powered (and paying) career. How many young people ended up with degrees in exotic subjects, and then found they were unemployable because the available jobs didn't match up with their training?

"Environmental science" and "social behavior" are seen as important areas of knowledge. Much of what we experience in our cultural life (what creates our world view and places us securely in our time) is obsolete within our own lifetime. *Wisdom is better than beauty. Immortality is an illusion. Eternity is real.*

Books (novels)....the classics...*tales of greatness and desperation*...truth revealed in stories of men and women doing the right thing for the right reason...the heroic stand against evil, even unto death, of courage and sacrifice. We share in the eternal moment even as we confront our real human fear of dying. We speak up for what is right. We choose to do good work. We do not live by natural instincts.

My father looms large in my eyes for his accomplishments and for overcoming hardship and impossible circumstances, even though he never wrote a book or became a famous artist. Real heroes become heroes by the choices they make. The unsung heroes aren't trying to escape *from* their lives.

They seek the meaning of why they lived in the temporal moment given to them. The desire to live within the boundaries of being caring humans is truly heroic.

Hans Jordac was a director of an orphanage in Belgium when the Nazis invaded his country. The Nazi "Operation T-4" was to "cleanse" Europe of all children whose lineage could not be verified and were accordingly deemed genetically inferior. Jordac was relieved of his post and told to leave. He refused.

The Nazi in charge tried to offer him mercy: "Go, forget these children. They are no longer your responsibility."

"They are my children. Whatever you do to them, you must do to me also."

"Don't you understand?" The Nazi pleaded with him. "They are all being sent to a camp to be… eliminated."

"Then, send me with them. Wherever they go, I go."

Hans Jordac died in a concentration camp with *his* children.

Chapter Nineteen

My mother's conversion from atheism wasn't due to religious belief but as a result of an after-death experience. In 1983 she suffered heart failure at fifty years old. She was rushed to the hospital emergency room and arrived clinically dead where she was revived with electric paddles. She related her story, which was quite similar to so many other accounts.

She looked down at her body on the gurney and saw the doctors working to revive her. She was encompassed by a bright light and began walking along a pathway toward its source. She was met by a soft-spoken man, also radiating a beneficent, comforting light. He told her, in a soothing voice, that she had died and that all her troubles in life were at an end. He was taking her to a place of perfect peace. She began walking with him into the tunnel. As they walked, she felt she wasn't ready to go with him and asked the man if she'd see her husband and children again.

"Not for a long time," he replied. "They aren't

making the journey now."

"What if I don't want to go?" she asked.

"If that's what you choose, it's okay…but the way back is harder than the way forward. If you go back you will be in your body which has been damaged by a very bad heart condition. But if you want to go back…you can."

"I'll see my children again? And my husband?"

"Yes."

"Then, I want to go back."

At that point she found herself watching the doctors applying the paddles to her body, she felt the zap rush through her entire being and then she dropped back into her body, opened her eyes, and heard one of the doctors say, "We have a pulse. She's going to make it."

Rose and I returned from Baja because my mother was about to undergo open-heart surgery. We were there to lend emotional support and help in her recovery. We sat with my father in a private waiting room for six hours. My father wept and prayed. During that vigil, I held his hand and kept saying, "She's going to make it."

A few hours after surgery, she regained consciousness and we were allowed to see her for a few minutes. She wasn't groggy but did look like she'd been through an ordeal of unimaginable suffering. I hugged her and she smiled.

"I was never afraid," she stated emphatically. "I know there's nothing to be afraid of. This life is the pathway to eternal life. I know, I was allowed to see that death is not the end. Heaven is waiting. There is a god."

Her heart troubles began when she was afflicted with scarlet fever as a young girl. Then, the death of her first-born son, Lenny (my older brother), beset her with unending grief.

The open-heart surgery and quadruple bypass was a complete success. She recovered and lived a fairly active life until age sixty-seven, when she suffered a brain hemorrhage in her sleep. She was transferred to the Mary Hitchcock Center in Dartmouth N.H. where she was kept alive for two days on life-support. Blood vessels in her brain had "leaked" into the lobe that controls blood pressure. Her heart was still beating with the strength of a seventeen-year-old.

My younger brother, my father, and myself drove to Dartmouth intending to disconnect her from life support, but she expired moments before we actually pulled the plug. My father kissed her hands and feet. Then he looked at me and said, "I feel very sad for you boys. You just lost the best friend you're ever going to have."

Chapter Twenty

I had never really submitted or surrendered to the underlying requirement to give up my life to the authority that underscored the belief system of the Twelve Tribes. I was still "sovereign" of my own life. What kept me from leaving "the community" was my own belief that I was living in an environment that allowed for I-YOU relationships to exist as an active phenomenon of the social life I had definitely experienced in the Twelve Tribes. No one in the community watched television. The world of IT simply did not seem to matter. No news. No vacations. No ambitions to obscure the vital realities that dominated the inner dimensions of a very real and profoundly sequestered life of living for each other. The Twelve Tribes preaches how to defeat evil and bring about "the end of the age" by sharing in a common life.

Since I functioned as a public relations expert, I was afforded unlimited mobility to travel between many communities, more than ten. I was put in charge of press conferences, public forums, stage plays, concert tours, and other major events. I wrote some content for the Twelve Tribes website. I formed an intimate relationship with the group's leader and "apostle," Eugene Spriggs.

From my earliest encounters with him, and onwards for a number of years, I came to regard him as an absolutely sincere believer and most affable (if not eccentric) man. He was well-read and intensely communicative. He had been a guidance counselor and a devout Christian in the 1970s. He gathered around him a dedicated band of seekers who had unswerving loyalty to their cause. In Chattanooga, they formed "The Light Brigade" and established a number of cafés under the name "Yellow Deli." In the late 70s, he made a strategic decision to move his entire church to Island Pond, Vermont. From there, they established a worldwide "commonwealth" or "confederacy" of twenty or so communities with several thousand members in nine countries.

Nine/Eleven. The Twelve Tribes Communities sponsored a crew of EMTs, all "disciples" of Yahshua, to travel to Manhattan in their camper-bus, The Peacemaker. At various venues, the bus was a presence instantly recognized by both fans and detractors.

The Twelve Tribes had contracted to work for Phish at IT and Coventry, at Moe Down, BerkFest, Shamballah, and had set up field hospitals for such colossal events as Bonnaroo in Tennessee as well as touring behind The Grateful Dead, Widespread Panic, and Bob Dylan. The Twelve Tribes had earned a respectable reputation administering first aid. The medical contingent was FEMA-approved and on call, so within hours of the attack on the World Trade Center, the bus was on the scene. I was on board as a grief counselor. The bus transported people who were forced to leave their apartments until all the buildings could be inspected for damage. Hundreds of people were bused out of their neighborhoods to temporary shelters. After that, we were permitted by the local authorities to park the bus at Cooper Union Square for ten days.

Three of my daughters were married by 2005. My youngest daughter was still living with me in a Twelve Tribes community in Ithaca. My oldest daughter was living there as well, with her husband and my grandson. I'd reached a place in my own development that I could no longer accept the confinement and lack of personal growth that overwhelmed me. I felt unfulfilled, lonely, and no longer able or willing to go along with the agenda of the Twelve Tribes. I left the community knowing I could never return or go along with what they believed. My youngest daughter wanted to stay with her sister, and I agreed to allow her to make that choice. She was fifteen years old.

***

December 2006. My father, at eighty-six, lived through heart surgery but was given an aspirin derivative after the operation which caused his kidneys to fail. I rushed to his bedside in Florida. He looked more like a child than an old, shrunken man. Just as I arrived, he regained consciousness. He opened his eyes and spoke, saying, "You're here. I love you. And I can still throw a one-two punch and lick any man who needs it."

He did not recover. For two weeks, I spoon-fed him baby food. But every other day, he underwent dialysis.

Finally, he told me, "Take me home. Unplug me from the damn machine. I want out." He lived for another ten days in an unconscious state, under the care of Hospice, peacefully at rest, on a gurney in the living room of his apartment.

One afternoon, in those last days, he woke up for a few minutes while I was playing my guitar and singing one of my songs. He smiled and said, "I like your song." And then he closed his eyes, turned inward, and sank into an ever-deeper sleep. And finally, he expired in the silent peace of his own choosing. At age sixty, I became an orphan. My father was the last of the Lavin clan, the last of an entire generation who had shaped the history of the 20th century. My elders, from whom I had come, were gone.

Chapter Twenty-One

From 2007 through 2008, I lived on the road in a teardrop camper pulled along by my van. I was homeless by choice—or, more accurately, home on the road. I arranged a formidable schedule of poetry readings and gigs. I wasn't making much more than would cover expenses, but I worked in Austin, Texas; Ocracoke, North Carolina; Logan, Utah; Ft. Lauderdale, Florida; Bennington, Vermont; and Washington D.C.

I toured the vast outlands of Montana, camped along the Big Sur, slept in the deserts, ferried to the outer banks, and finally went back to Florida to live near the ocean. I rented a small studio space, where I wrote *God's People*, and then the novel *Crooked River/Black Mountain*.

I visited Rosemary's grave in 2010. Years of grieving and a deep emptiness gripped me. The years had not expunged the devastating loss I'd internalized. I had never really found peace or been able to move on. Our life together, the evolution of our love for each other, had been tumultuous, complete, and finalized in the epiphany of her death.

I could not see a way out of the grief that consumed me. Death beckoned and my health deteriorated. I stopped eating and was drinking myself into oblivion, living on whiskey and candy bars. But there was no way back, no remedy to save me. Plainly, I had internalized the deep loss I felt. All those years of fighting to save Rosemary had ended with unresolved and incomprehensible separation. That was dramatically revealed while on a trip to Washington D.C., when I went for a cup of coffee at the Space Museum canteen. I was brought back to a vivid memory of when we had been in this exact place together. All at once I began to weep, heaving and sobbing, as hundreds of people sat about me sipping their drinks and eating their sandwiches. Who could save me from my own internal workings? At that moment, I was rendered a helpless idiot unable to be consoled. I was alone in a place "like stone carved from memory."

In those last months of her life, Rosemary and I spent hours upon hours discussing all that we'd done, all that we'd learned, all that we'd shared. We came to see how our love had survived, and we had passed through our fears and anxieties to become inseparable. We had survived the world, together. She was sleeping most of the day and then would be awake and alert between 1 a.m. and 5 a.m. In those hours, we found our joy, our intimacy, our togetherness. And we had found the strength to face what had now become the obvious, the inevitable end that we could not change, nor prevent, nor escape. The doctor had explained to us that as her disease progressed, she would need more liquid opium (this in addition to the steady doses she absorbed from opium patches).

Our second marriage brought us to a sobering apex in life. I was fifty-five. Rosemary was forty-seven. Our oldest son flew up from Florida. For us, as parents, this was essentially a reconciliation with him and for him. And his time to say good-bye to his mother. When he arrived, Rosemary and I were sitting on our bed.

She spoke first. "Son, I want you to believe what I'm going to say. If I had known then what I know now, I never would have left your father." He stared lovingly into her eyes and nodded in agreement and satisfaction. In any case, it was a deeply healing moment.

And then I said, "Son, if I had known then what I know now, I never would have let your mother leave."

Our marriage had boosted her spirits, but she was still weak because she wasn't keeping food down. She had been living on oatmeal water and soda crackers. Someone suggested I read *The Zone Diet*, which proved a crucial adjustment. I shopped and cooked for her needs, both of us eating poached salmon, avocado, soft boiled eggs, and a modicum of fresh vegetables and fruits. Her appetite returned, and she ate three meals a day for the ensuing six months. She was getting stronger again. We were happy to be together, and both of us had a renewed hope that we still had a chance to get through her ordeals.

Rosemary had been bedridden ever since she slipped in the mud back in December. She lamented how she would never walk again, no longer able to get fifty steps out to the garden to sit in the sun or leave her bed. I got in touch with a renowned Feldenkrais practitioner, a therapist I'd worked with, and with whom I'd had a professional friendship for more than thirty years. I explained the situation. He suggested I get Rosemary a set of Alpine walking sticks. I hiked into the woods across from the farmhouse and cut two pieces of oak to the right length to fit my wife's frame, padded the tops with sponge wrapped in felt, bought two rubber caps (the kind used for canes) and presented them to my wife.

We started slowly, with a very limited expectation. Out of the bed, and on her feet. She could get to the bathroom for a shower, where I set up a chair for her to sit on in the tub. A week later, she got to the porch and sat watching the garden grow. In late May, I set up a chair in the garden, and she was able to walk out the door, down a few steps, and sit for an hour or so. We usually had our lunch outside in the sun and fresh air. How wonderful that was.

Then, one day in early June, she got outside expecting to sit for a while but there was no chair. "Sholom, where's my chair?"

"There." I was pointing to our car in the driveway, the door open. "I've packed our lunch. We're going on a picnic!"

We drove to the highest point between Salem, New York and Dorset, Vermont, and there, with a panoramic view of twenty miles, in the lush greenery of an Edenic landscape, we gazed to the far distance, where a lake shimmered with speckles of sunlight in pastoral peace.

During those final days of our life together, we made several outings to waterfalls, and into the Adirondacks, to the Great Sacandaga. Our last road trip was a most adventurous ride to Desolation Lake, thirty miles from anywhere. On that ride, Rosemary collapsed, and I raced us back to the farm. After that, we never ventured more than a few miles from home.

Rosemary wrote one poem during that time. Being a visual artist, she spent many of her days drawing or painting. It was the only poem she wrote.

From a California Girl: To Daddy

1.

It was Easter. You took us to Death Valley.
I was six.
We hardly ever saw you. It was special, exciting.
Death Valley must be someplace grand.
With you it was always grand.
We all went, your whole, big family.
Six children and your wife.
To Death Valley, in a pink Rambler station wagon.
It was 1958. The desert was hot in the sun.
We walked. It was Easter morning.
I had red sneakers on with white rubber tips.
We all wore pants and walked through the sandy,
dry, hot desert.
Sage brush, tumbleweed, rocks, cactus.
A hot wind. No one else was there.
You told us to watch where we stepped in case a
snake was there.
The sun grew hotter. My head pounded.
We came to an unusual place. The rocks got bigger.
There were little ledges.

And a bridge formed from the rock.
"A natural bridge," you called it. All rock.
Not one living thing on it. Tan in color, bleached
earth by the blazing sun.

2.

We went back to the motel.
We swam in the pool.
Then we got dressed up in special dresses,
suits and fancy shoes.
We hunted for turquoise, pink and yellow eggs
in the motel yard.

3.

On the ride home I pressed my face against your
sweaty neck
as you drove, standing behind you.
"Daddy," I said.
"Yes."
"I don't want to grow up..."
"Why don't you want to grow up?"
"I don't want to be selfish. All day I just kept
thinking about myself."
"What do you mean?"
"Like about my new dress and my new shoes. Now
I feel bad. I don't like it, Daddy. I just don't like
getting bigger. I never felt this way before."

"Just because you grow up doesn't mean you have
to become selfish, Rosie. In fact, the most important
thing is to remember others before yourself."

I wanted to cry because I believed you with all my heart.

I was *so* glad you said that. How much I loved you.

R. M. Lavin

***

Looking back, those were blissful days. Yes, Rosemary was hurting and the specter of her illness was always upon us. But life, so precious, such a gift, and not be squandered, gave us focus. We were thankful for all we had, all we shared, all that had given our life together an intense meaning that was not lost to us.

But we were in a battle that took its toll on both of us. We had tried every reasonable treatment. We were worn down and out of answers. When Rose confided to me that she was ready to face the reality that she wasn't going to live much longer, I made inquiries about which doctors were trying cutting-edge experimental research in the field, and I made contact by phone with a doctor in France. He was willing to speak with me but hesitant to offer any concrete advice.

I explained how we had been battling her breast cancer for four years but had reached an impasse. We were desperately reaching out for any inkling of what we might still do.

We'd tried flax oil, juice fasts, goat's milk, and a live food diet. He asked me if this was a hoax, a prank call from his detractors or the media, but I assured him I was just a desperate man trying to save my wife. I would settle for any glimmer of hope. A new, experimental treatment, something, anything. I was pleading with him. Finally, he accepted what I was telling him to be true. His prognosis wasn't encouraging. If everything I had told him was accurate, and my wife had survived four years, he said, "You are ahead of me. You know more than I do." We had already beaten the odds. There was nothing else to be done.

My wife and I began serious conversations as to what we would do when the end seemed upon us. We formed a plan that when the pain was unbearable, and we would know when that time came, I would administer whatever dose she needed. If she was too weak to speak, we agreed on a signal…she would blink in a rapid burst to let me know she needed more medication.

The more fragile she became, the more my love for her intensified. We truly had become soul-mates. We had bonded in love over a twenty-five year lifetime. We had seen our children grow and become whole human beings.

And finally, we were facing death together. We ate our last meal a few days before she became too weak to wake up. She went into a coma and was on a breathing machine.

The only time she regained consciousness was to ask for more roxinal. Then, after ten days languishing in a comatose sleep, she opened her eyes.

"Do you need a drink?" I asked.

She could not speak. She blinked her eyes, rapidly, as if pleading for me to administer the medication to numb the pain. She was too weak to sit up. I held her and poured the medicine into her mouth. I put her head back on the pillow. Suddenly, she sat up and looked deeply into my eyes. She spoke my name, "Sholom."

I gently embraced her and put my mouth to her ear. As she took her last breath, I whispered, "You are so beautiful. I love you so much. I am thankful for the life we had."

Afterword

I chose to be a writer and poetry was my medium. I was trained in the Objectivist shadow of George Oppen, and by the sober sensibility of Jon Silkin, my two mentors. Many of my poems were derived from the meaning of life I cultivated and embraced while raising my children and loving my wife. Others were written to decry injustice and others to pierce the veil of totalitarian thought.

Poems are esoteric reflections of what is to be spoken beyond empirical meaning. Language evokes unspeakable mystery via an elusive artistic thought process, molded by craft and intellect. Concrete substance and conceptual being are joined.

Poetry evokes the primal mystery of the language external to what is known, a priori utterance of the human soul, the song of blood pumping and thought aspiring to become reality. And poems also express the triumph and tragedy and suffering and beauty of our human experience, captured in the spoken moment of conception, transforming human experience into existential revelation.

Poetry dares to speculate beyond the possible, what is attainable though never attained, the artifact of an energy belonging to anyone who desires to embrace eternity as the moment of being there. The poem takes us through the wormhole into the unknown.

Each poem stands as its own orchestration, and each poem succeeds or fails as an autonomous effort. But there is also a judgment that any reader is invited to make, a judgment based upon a consistency of craft. Beyond competence, I have always believed the poet is responsible to project a convincing epical journey, through real-life experiences communicated in a common language that real people can understand.

Authentic poetry meets a real human need. A poem can decry injustice, or celebrate life, or reveal secrets heretofore not known. The poem can also be a mysterious evocation of mystery, and ultimately the prophetic voice of the poet ought to be the conduit for that mystery.

OM TAT SAT OM

One must not come to feel that you have a thousand threads in your hand
   You must see the one thing
   There are many levels
   But there is only one level of Art
   You must see the one thing

— George Oppen

Poems

S. R. Lavin

THEY KNEW ME WHEN

Sleeping in the forest
with my infant son

a journey of self
into life and death,
alone in the wilderness
left to me by the Indians,
restating their poetry
to dramatize my own.

A man and a woman
establish
the boundaries of love
and disillusionment.

Sparrows sing.

Buildings wall up the landscape.

Snuggled to my son
in the early morning mist
I forget I write poetry...

The wind blows my words away.

HARPO MARX &
The Last Days of the Warsaw Ghetto

we were like fog in the ghetto
it was a harp without strings
we were tone deaf

we are required to butcher the young cows
they shiver—rear up like a rodeo
they cloak themselves in animal moans
their throats snap
two or three cows back from
the executioner

they roll their cigars in their teeth
they plot where the ashes fall
the ones in white coats

how to get the seed out of itself

you wade into the sewers up to your neck

it was the only way out
in those days

in those days

a rodeo was all we had

HIRAM Poetry Review, 1972

S. R. Lavin

BIG WADI

The unspeakable, who can say
what is not these words, yet
what it is can be said
this way: Light changes utterly
the darkness, within one's self,
all capacity, all capability
so that the richest truth
lies in the darkest parts,
the words hewn of
silent repentance,
sorting out what's so
from what isn't,
etching the time into
something comprehensible.
It's in me and then
I notice it's missing.

Nothing diminishes sacrifice.

It takes a lifetime
to see the little parts
add up to something.

Here's where I rest, at the edge
of rolling hills and timberline,
a thousand hills, a thousand miles,
a thousand little ponds and creeks.

Vermont Poetry Review, 1996

CHICOPEE RIVER

Snakes a river plumed in azaleas
and I remember the Indians
named this place
Chicopee.

Wild azaleas and their reflection,
reflects the nature of the moment
more than of time or its content.

We live in the reflections,
in their own way
as real as the blossoms
then as now

sheds self for life after life
(not reflected but
the measured pace
of substance)

bigger than self

bigger than world

S. R. Lavin

THE FRENCH AND INDIAN WARS

What is and what isn't the French and Indian Wars,
governments collapsing upon themselves, like bats
folding their wings, covers the truth with darkness.

Between battles we idle by the river on a summer
day, sucking on blades of grass and feeling the sun
make us over.

The nation hoods its citizens, gasses us,
maligns our truths and our dignity,
leaving only us, the collected evil and good
that exists in all places at all times.

Eternal flame, fallen President—fallen country.

Here my moment of silence extends beyond any one
victim. I respond to jungle, stalking myself, hunting
for words.

I am the distance Time travels, images of Heaven,
the re-images of our failures and our successes.
I am the conscience of a nation.

Unable to prevent History I become it.

Springfield Journal, Springfield, Mass. 1983

AMERICAN CONCERT

River bends by ducks and herons, the wilderness.
Sky with fresh water, the air has a sweetness.
Okeechobee, ancient god of the glades, not
crocodile, but parrot-man.

Through me, male beaking her neck, and erect,
I enter her.

Poachers come for the feathers. Polluted highway
and broken glass. "To live is hard, to die is harder."
Sunset follows sunset. My god calls to me.

Thunder—the thunder of the highways—the
thunder of America. One day becomes another.

On August 23rd, in 1937,
in Charlestown Massachusetts,
Sacco and Vanzetti were electrocuted.   '
They were immigrants and anarchists.

The dead live in a mountain of tangled endings.
One more day. One more day.

This is what we get for gunning down our President,
the endless thunder of the highway, the trucks
farting out their poisons.

Smiling in the face of discomfort and certain death
the new President wants another war.

The black thunder of dying.

S. R. Lavin

THE RUSTED ARM OF GOD

Eternity surrounds us—
(Time as illusion)

the revelation

that life and death
flow together,

a glimpse of sparkle
in the crystallized dew drops
of the waking world.

Strength, not weakness,
wrings out the truth.

These words from isolation:
<u>to suffer is to know</u>

(not religion
but sacrifice).

Beyond understanding—

the immortal song of a grasshopper
on a warm summer day.

Vermont Literary Review, 1997

PERDIDO

Alone in a place where no one breathes
I sleep like stone carved from memory.

I've lost in myself what belongs to others.

We lose another President.

From failure, collapse.
From collapse, void.

Night brings the truth back to me,
what could be called peace,
to know something of one's self
not previously known.

Each morning the dead are collected
from the pavement. They are not counted.
They have no names.

Wealth without justice
condemns the innocent
with the guilty.

All that should be right is wrong.
All that can be done has not been done.

Among the dead are those we love
and those we never know.
How could we?

"We are corrupt. We are losing our soul."

There is the cold clarity of despair.

The streets are dirty.

Promises have been broken.

STAND Magazine, 1983

CONTOOCOOK

(Those who were here are not here now.)

We are defined by what we do
but what we do is not who we are—

untouchable jet stream
thread human connectedness

such finality, when life (as we know it)

whooshed backwards

(all gone who lived before)

and those now living
disappeared

transported souls

pin-pointed disillusionment:
quaint quietude schmoozed
into big buck condo homelessness.

On one side
human need,

on the other—

glistening and eternal

S. R. Lavin

BIG MEADOW / NEW RIVER

Non-simultaneous
only partially overlapping
the universe is what we say it is,
the parts greater than the whole.

I naked, climbed to a high place
overlooking the world and
dreamed my death there.

Something so animal
you pay for it
if necessary.

Earth. Word
and vocabulary.

The Earth has
its own music
based in eternity
and plays that theme:

you go for a walk
you don't come back.

I want Mine.

I want Oil.

I want Television.

Dying and being born.
This is who we are.

The news is ATTICA.

A MOUNTAIN OUTSIDE
my window.

Electricity,
I wrote
where
he
painted
yellow.

Outside myself:
pistol flame
from hyacinth
arose stamen.

Take none of this:
much of what you think
stones are alive.

Corpses strewn
on every beach,
each shot in the head.

They were fanatics.

The ocean swallowed them.

Soft coral antlers die in the sun.

S. R. Lavin

Bone by day, shells
for my necklace

Jerusalem House, 1979

From the Book Called
AMERICA

In the lost country of the Berkshires,
somewhere near Peru, Massachusetts
I fall asleep not knowing
if I will ever wake up.

Passing along the bogs and swampy bottoms
(these places have haunting beauty)
I remember what my friend said
the last time I saw him, "Life
is sweet gravy." A few days later
he killed himself.
He was dying of cancer
and didn't want to suffer
anymore or have his family
bear the expense of useless treatments.

I stare across the mountains
to the distant past, seeing as clearly now
as when my wife and I
skirted along the ancient riverbeds
and came to Ignacio, where our love
became eternal
among the thousands of years
of history we had stumbled upon.

In the book called *AMERICA*
the truth is written
on the painted cliff walls.
The miles of black volcanic rock
are the timeless witness.

In the book it is written:

This is eternity...welcome home.

Voice in the Whirlwind, SynergEBooks, 2009

About the Author

Born in 1945, S. R. Lavin has been widely published since 1967 in the U.S. as well as internationally in England, China, Poland, Israel, Japan and the Netherlands. Among his books are Let Myself Shine (Kulchur Press, 1979), *The Stonecutters at War With the Cliff Dwellers* (Heron Press, 1971), *Voice in the Whirlwind* (Poems, 1979-2007), SynergEBooks, 2007), *Metacomet: The Saga of King Philip* (SynergEBooks, 2007), *ECTO* (SynergEBooks, 2009), *God's People in Search of a Destiny, a provocative look at life inside The Twelve Tribes Communities* (SynergEBooks, 2006), *Journey to a Lone Star* (Four Zoas Press, 1976), *Big Meadow / New River* (Jerusalem House, 1978) and *PERDIDO* (a folio of nine poems), printed by the poet in a limited edition.

S. R. Lavin was founding editor and publisher of *The Four Zoas Journal of Poetry and Letters*, a five-time recipient of N.E.A. Grants in Literature (USA, 1972-1980) and winner of the Leonardo da Vinci Cultural Achievement Award (Florence, Italy). He was a creative writing teacher at several colleges in

Vermont and was a poet-in-residence at Clark University and Northampton School for Girls. He has taught Creative Writing, Literature, given writing workshops and has performed in numerous colleges, as well as at The Knitting Factory (NYC) and the Iron Horse (Northampton, Mass.) and at coffee houses, galleries, and art centers.

Sholom Roy Lavin (Stuart Roy Lavin) passed away January 12, 2019. His books are still available on Amazon and through Lady June Press.

Also Available From Lady June Press

Historical Fiction

MAHAT
Or, the Essence of Being
by S. R. Lavin

Fiction and Poetry

The Velvet-Lined Toilet Bowl
Featuring I and You: An Original Poemic Transliteration
by S. R. Lavin

Nonfiction / Martial Arts

Sphere of Influence: An Approach to Self-Defense
by M. D. Holden and Rosa Sophia

The Fighter Within: A Fighter's Life
by Isaiah Gathings, Sr.

www.ingramcontent.com/pod-product-compliance
Lightning Source LLC
Chambersburg PA
CBHW072344090426
42741CB00012B/2918